DENNIS FRANK

"Master Life"

growth. wisdom. balance.

AI UNVEILED

Navigating the Intersection of Technology, Ethics, and Society

DENNIS FRANK

Copyright Notice

This book is intended to provide accurate and authoritative information about Artificial Intelligence. It is sold with the understanding that neither the author nor the publisher is offering professional advice on AI development, programming, or its implementation in specific professional fields. If expert assistance in AI or related technologies is required, the services of a qualified professional should be sought. This is an informational resource and should not be used as a sole guide for AI-related projects or decisions.

Produced in the United States of America

KRYPTOKRAKEN™ PRODUCTIONS

DEDICATION

This book is dedicated to Eva, my wife, for all her love, understanding, and patience. She has blessed me enormously.

Preface

Welcome to my exploration of Artificial Intelligence. This course is crafted to simplify and demystify AI, making it approachable and understandable for everyone. AI, in my view, is a powerful tool that can significantly enhance various professional fields like psychology, science, and surgery, aiding experts to be more skilled and knowledgeable.

However, it's important to clarify my stance on the integration of AI into the physical human body. While I recognize and appreciate the potential of AI in augmenting human capabilities, I am not an advocate for the creation of a new race of part-machine, part-human beings. The focus of this course is on AI as an external, supportive technology, not as an intrinsic part of our physical selves.

My goal is to present AI as a technology that, when used responsibly, can bring immense benefits to humanity. It's about leveraging AI to enhance our skills and understanding, not about blurring the lines between human and machine on a physical or biological level.

As we journey through this course together, let's keep an open mind about the incredible potential of AI, while also being mindful of the ethical boundaries and the importance of maintaining our human essence.

Welcome to a world of learning and discovery.

Dennis Frank

"The beauty of AI lies in its ability to learn; the beauty of humanity in its ability to teach." - Dennis Frank

"In the dance of human progress, AI is our most intriguing partner – leading us into seemingly endless possibilities and unforeseen challenges. Embrace the moment, and let innovation lead the way."
- Dennis Frank

Table of Contents

"Within the intricate web of our modern world, AI is the silent weaver – crafting a tapestry of change and innovation. It's our task to understand its threads, shaping a future that harmonizes technology with the essence of humanity." - Dennis Frank

1.1 Introduction to Artificial Intelligence

Welcome to the fascinating world of Artificial Intelligence (AI). This lesson serves as your gateway to understanding this transformative technology that is subtly revolutionizing our world.

Understanding the term Artificial Intelligence

Artificial Intelligence, often simply referred to as AI, is a broad branch of computer science that aims to simulate human intelligence in machines. It is about designing machines capable of thinking like humans and performing tasks such as learning, problem-solving, perception, language understanding, and decision-making.

AI is not a system, but it is implemented in the system. For example, while a system like a robot can be called AI, it's the programming and algorithms that allow it to operate autonomously that truly embody the concept of AI.

The basic components of AI: Machine Learning and Deep Learning

AI is a vast field, but two of its most fundamental components are Machine Learning (ML) and Deep Learning (DL).

Machine Learning is a subset of AI that involves the creation of algorithms that allow machines to learn from data and make decisions or predictions. In other words, ML enables machines to improve their performance without being explicitly programmed to do so.

Deep Learning, on the other hand, is a subset of ML that uses artificial neural networks with several layers (hence the 'deep' in Deep Learning) to model and understand complex patterns in datasets. This technology is the driving force behind innovations like self-driving cars and voice assistants.

Brief history and evolution of AI

The concept of AI is not a new one. The idea of creating machines capable of mimicking human intelligence dates back to antiquity. However, it wasn't until the 20th century, with the advent of modern computers, that AI became a tangible field of research.

The term "Artificial Intelligence" was first coined by John McCarthy in 1956 during the Dartmouth Conference, where the core mission of AI — to create machines as intelligent as humans — was proposed.

Since then, AI has evolved dramatically. In the 1990s and early 2000s, Machine Learning emerged as a crucial component of AI, thanks largely to the availability of digital data and the development of the internet. More recently, Deep Learning has taken the AI world by storm, driven by advancements in data storage, computing power, and neural networks.

In conclusion, AI is a transformative technology that's been decades in the making. Its applications are vast, and its potential is enormous. As we delve deeper into this course, we'll explore the many facets of AI, its implications, and the future it holds in various sectors.

"Artificial Intelligence will reach human levels by around 2029. Follow that out further to, say, 2045, we will have multiplied the intelligence, the human biological machine intelligence of our civilization a billion-fold." - Ray Kurzweil

1.2 The Core Concepts of AI

In this lesson, we will delve into the core concepts of Artificial Intelligence. We aim to break down complex AI terminologies into digestible content, providing a clear understanding of the fundamentals of AI.

Fundamentals of AI: Algorithms, Neural Networks, and AI Models

Artificial Intelligence, at its core, is about creating machines that can think, learn, and make decisions like humans. This is achieved through three fundamental components: Algorithms, Neural Networks, and AI Models.

Algorithms are a set of rules or instructions given to an AI system to help it learn from data. They play a crucial role in determining how an AI system will process data and make decisions.

Neural Networks, inspired by the human brain's structure, are a series of algorithms that work together to recognize patterns from data. They are the backbone of many AI applications, enabling systems to learn and improve over time.

AI Models are the output of trained algorithms and neural networks. They are the final product that can make predictions or decisions based on the data they have learned from.

Understanding AI Terminologies: Supervised Learning, Unsupervised Learning, Reinforcement Learning

AI is often categorized into three main types of learning: Supervised Learning, Unsupervised Learning, and Reinforcement Learning.

Supervised Learning is a type of machine learning where an AI system is trained using labeled data. In other words, the system is given a dataset where the correct answers (or labels) are already known, and it learns to predict the correct answer for new data.

Unsupervised Learning, on the other hand, involves training an AI system using data that is not labeled. The system must find patterns and relationships in the data on its own, which can be more complex but also allows for more unexpected insights.

Reinforcement Learning is a type of machine learning where an AI system learns to make decisions by trial and error. The system is rewarded or penalized for its actions, and over time, it learns to make the best decisions to maximize its reward.

The Role of Data in AI

Data is the lifeblood of AI. It's the fuel that powers every AI system. Without data, AI systems cannot learn, make predictions, or improve their performance.

In AI, data is used for training, testing, and validating models. Training data helps AI systems learn and create models. Testing data is used to evaluate the model's performance, and validation data is used to fine-tune the model.

Remember, the quality and quantity of data directly impact the performance of an AI system. The more high-quality data an AI system has, the better it can learn and make accurate predictions.

In the next lesson, we will explore the various applications of AI in everyday life. We will discuss how AI is subtly revolutionizing our world and how it's becoming an invisible part of our daily lives.

In the meantime, feel free to go over the lesson again to solidify your understanding of the core concepts of AI. Remember, understanding these fundamentals is key to demystifying AI and embracing the AI revolution.

1.3 AI Applications in Everyday Life

Artificial Intelligence (AI) has become an integral part of our daily lives, often without us even realizing it. It is subtly influencing our decisions, behaviors, and interactions, marking an invisible revolution in how we live, work, and play. This lesson will explore some of the ways AI is seamlessly integrating into our world.

How AI Subtly Influences Our Daily Life

AI has the unique ability to learn from experience, adjust to new inputs, and perform human-like tasks. From voice-powered personal assistants like Siri and Alexa to more complex technologies like behavioral algorithms, autonomous cars, and predictive search, AI is progressing rapidly. It's not just about robots anymore; AI is subtly embedded in your phones, cars, banks, and even your home.

Examples of AI in Everyday Use

Let's delve into some examples of how AI is used in our everyday lives:

1. **Virtual Assistants**: Siri, Alexa, and Google Assistant are all AI-powered virtual assistants that we interact with daily. They help us find information, remind us of our schedules, and even control our home appliances. These virtual assistants use AI to understand

our commands, learn our preferences, and provide personalized responses.

2. **Recommendation Systems**: Ever wondered how Netflix knows what movies you might like? Or how Amazon seems to know what you might want to buy next? The answer lies in AI-powered recommendation systems. These systems use machine learning algorithms to analyze your behavior and preferences, providing personalized recommendations that enhance your shopping or viewing experience.

3. **Autonomous Vehicles**: AI is at the heart of the revolution in autonomous vehicles. Companies like Tesla, Google, and Uber are using AI to teach cars how to navigate roads, recognize obstacles, and make decisions that were once solely the domain of human drivers.

The Invisible Revolution: AI Seamlessly Integrating into Our World

The true revolution of AI lies in its invisibility. It's not about robots taking over the world; it's about AI becoming a part of our everyday lives in ways we may not even notice. From the way we communicate, shop, watch movies, to how we drive, AI is subtly and seamlessly integrating into our world, making our lives easier, more efficient, and more connected.

In conclusion, AI is no longer a futuristic concept; it's here, and it's subtly revolutionizing our daily lives. As we move forward, AI will continue to evolve, becoming even more integrated into our world. The invisible revolution is well underway, and it's exciting to imagine what the future holds.

In the next lesson, we will explore AI's applications in different sectors, further highlighting the pervasive influence of this transformative technology.

" The language of AI is not just code, but a narrative of our evolving relationship with technology."
- Dennis Frank

1.4 AI in Different Sectors

Artificial Intelligence (AI) has been a game-changer in various sectors, transforming traditional processes, enhancing efficiency, and paving the way for innovation. This lesson will provide an overview of how AI has been applied in different sectors, including Healthcare, Finance, Retail, Entertainment, and Education. We will also discuss the transformative power of AI and provide case studies of successful AI implementation.

Healthcare

AI has revolutionized the healthcare sector by improving diagnosis, treatment planning, patient care, and administration. Machine learning algorithms can analyze vast amounts of data to identify patterns that can help in early disease detection. For instance, Google's DeepMind Health is being used to spot early signs of age-related macular degeneration and diabetic retinopathy.

Finance

In the finance sector, AI is used for algorithmic trading, fraud detection, customer service, and risk management. Robo-advisors, powered by AI, are providing personalized financial advice to customers. AI algorithms can analyze market trends and make trading decisions in a fraction of a second. For instance, JPMorgan's Contract Intelligence (COiN) platform uses machine learning to review legal documents and extract important data points and clauses.

Retail

AI has transformed the retail industry by personalizing the customer experience, managing inventory, and streamlining logistics. AI-powered chatbots are now common in online retail platforms, providing instant customer service. Amazon's AI-powered system anticipates customer needs and manages inventory in real-time.

Entertainment

In the entertainment industry, AI is used for content recommendation, audience analysis, and content creation. Netflix uses AI algorithms to recommend shows based on user behavior. AI is also being used to create music, write scripts, and even generate deepfake videos.

Education

AI is reshaping education by providing personalized learning experiences, automating administrative tasks, and even grading student work. Intelligent tutoring systems adapt to the learning style of each student, providing customized instruction and feedback. For instance, Carnegie Learning's MATHia platform uses AI to provide personalized math instruction.

Case Studies of Successful AI Implementation

Let's delve into some real-life examples of how AI has been successfully implemented in various sectors.

1. **Google's DeepMind Health in Healthcare**: DeepMind's AI system can analyze eye scans and spot early signs of age-related macular degeneration and

diabetic retinopathy, leading to early intervention and treatment.

2. **JPMorgan's COiN in Finance**: COiN uses machine learning to review and extract relevant data from legal documents in seconds, which would otherwise take hours of human work.

3. **Amazon's AI in Retail**: Amazon uses AI to predict customer behavior, manage inventory, and enhance the overall customer experience.

4. **Netflix's Recommendation Engine in Entertainment**: Netflix's AI algorithms analyze user behavior and preferences to recommend shows and movies, enhancing user engagement and satisfaction.

5. **Carnegie Learning's MATHia in Education**: MATHia uses AI to provide personalized math instruction, adapting to each student's learning style and pace, leading to improved learning outcomes.

In conclusion, AI has transformed and continues to revolutionize various sectors. As we move forward, the influence of AI will only become more pervasive, leading to more efficient processes, innovative solutions, and enhanced user experiences.

1.5 The Evolution of AI: From Concept to Revolution

In this lesson, we will trace the evolution of AI from its conceptual beginnings to the revolutionary force it is today. We will explore the key milestones that have shaped AI and examine how technological advancements have accelerated the AI revolution.

Tracing the Journey of AI: From its Inception to its Current State

AI, as a concept, has been part of human imagination for centuries, with ancient myths and stories often featuring non-human entities with intelligence. However, the scientific pursuit of AI began in earnest in the mid-20th century. The term "Artificial Intelligence" was first coined by John McCarthy in 1956 during the Dartmouth Conference, where the foundation for AI research was laid.

In the early years, AI research was focused on problem-solving and symbolic methods. This era, often referred to as the "Golden Age" of AI, saw the development of the first AI programs that could mimic human problem-solving skills.

The late 20th century brought a shift in AI research towards using statistical models and data-driven approaches, spurred by the availability of digital data and improvements in computational power. This period also saw the development of machine learning, a subfield of AI where computers learn from data.

The 21st century has witnessed an AI boom, with advancements in technologies such as deep learning and neural networks. Today, AI is not just a field of research but a practical reality, influencing various sectors from healthcare to finance, and from entertainment to education.

Key Milestones in the Evolution of AI

AI's journey has been marked by several key milestones. Here are a few notable ones:

- **1950**: Alan Turing proposed the Turing Test to measure a machine's ability to exhibit intelligent behavior.

- **1956**: The Dartmouth Conference where the term "Artificial Intelligence" was coined.

- **1965**: The development of ELIZA, the first chatbot, by Joseph Weizenbaum.

- **1980**: The rise of expert systems, computer systems that emulate the decision-making ability of a human expert.

- **1997**: IBM's Deep Blue defeats world chess champion Garry Kasparov.

- **2011**: IBM's Watson wins the game show Jeopardy, marking a significant achievement in natural language processing.

- **2012**: Google's neural network teaches itself to recognize cats in YouTube videos, a significant milestone in deep learning.

- **2014**: The development of chatbot platforms and personal assistants like Siri and Alexa.

- **2016**: Google's AlphaGo defeats world champion Go player Lee Sedol.

The Role of Technological Advancements in Accelerating the AI Revolution

Technological advancements have played a crucial role in accelerating the AI revolution. The exponential increase in computational power, the availability of large datasets, and advancements in algorithms have all contributed to the rapid progress of AI.

The development of Graphics Processing Units (GPUs) has significantly increased computational power, making it possible to process large amounts of data quickly. Similarly, the digitization of information has led to the availability of large datasets, which are essential for training AI systems.

Furthermore, advancements in algorithms, particularly in machine learning and deep learning, have enabled AI systems to learn from data and make predictions or decisions without being explicitly programmed.

In conclusion, the evolution of AI has been a journey of continuous learning and adaptation, driven by technological advancements and human ingenuity. Today, AI is a revolutionary force that is reshaping our world, offering immense possibilities for the future. As we continue to explore and understand this fascinating field, we are part of an exciting era of discovery and innovation.

In the next lesson, we will delve deeper into how AI has become an invisible revolution, subtly influencing various aspects of our lives.

1.6 AI: The Invisible Revolution

In this lesson, we will explore how Artificial Intelligence (AI) is subtly yet significantly revolutionizing our world, changing our lives, and shaping our future.

AI: The Subtle Revolution

Artificial Intelligence, often simply referred to as AI, is revolutionizing the world in ways that are not always immediately visible to the naked eye. It's an invisible revolution that's happening all around us, subtly but significantly altering how we live, work, and interact with the world.

From the smartphone in your hand that uses AI to optimize your user experience, to the online shopping platforms that recommend products based on your browsing history, AI is everywhere. It's in the email filters that keep your inbox spam-free, the voice assistants that help you manage your day, and the social media algorithms that curate your feeds.

The Societal Implications of the AI Revolution

The AI revolution is not just about technology; it's about society as a whole. AI is reshaping our societies in profound ways. It's changing how we communicate, how we work, how we learn, and even how we entertain ourselves.

In the world of work, AI is automating repetitive tasks, freeing up humans to focus on more complex and creative tasks. In education, AI is personalizing learning, providing students with tailored learning experiences that adapt to their individual needs and pace. In healthcare, AI is improving diagnosis and treatment, helping doctors to save lives and improve patient care.

However, the AI revolution also brings with it a host of societal challenges. As AI becomes more pervasive, issues around privacy, security, and ethics come to the fore. How do we ensure that AI is used responsibly? How do we protect our privacy in an age of AI? How do we ensure that the benefits of AI are distributed equitably? These are some of the questions that we will explore in later modules.

Conclusion

The AI revolution is here, and it's transforming our world in ways that are both visible and invisible. It's an exciting time, but also a time of great responsibility. As we continue to explore the world of AI in this course, we will delve deeper into these transformations, the opportunities they present, and the challenges they pose.

In the next lesson, we will look at the future of AI, exploring predictions and possibilities of what lies ahead in this exciting field.

Remember, the AI revolution may be invisible, but its impact is undeniable. As we navigate this new era, let's strive to harness the power of AI for the greater good, ensuring that this invisible revolution leads to visible progress for all.

1.7 AI and the Future: Predictions and Possibilities

In this lesson, we will explore the future predictions and possibilities of AI, discuss the opportunities and challenges it presents, and understand how it could revolutionize various industries. We will also discuss how we can prepare for a future dominated by AI.

Predictions about the Future of AI: Opportunities and Challenges

AI is poised to become a transformative technology of our time. As we move forward, the capabilities of AI are expected to continue to grow exponentially. Predictions about the future of AI range from optimistic to cautious.

On the optimistic side, AI is predicted to bring about significant improvements in various sectors. It could lead to more efficient processes, personalized services, and innovative solutions to complex problems. For example, in healthcare, AI could enable early detection of diseases and personalized treatment plans. In education, AI could provide personalized learning experiences and make quality education accessible to all.

However, the future of AI also presents several challenges. One of the main concerns is the impact of AI on jobs. While AI could create new jobs, it could also render some existing jobs obsolete. Another concern is the ethical implications of AI, such as privacy issues and the potential for AI to be used maliciously.

The Potential of AI to Revolutionize Various Industries

AI has the potential to revolutionize various industries, from healthcare and education to finance and retail. By automating routine tasks, AI could increase efficiency and productivity. By analyzing large amounts of data, AI could provide insights that help businesses make informed decisions.

In healthcare, AI could transform diagnosis, treatment, and patient care. In education, AI could personalize learning and improve student outcomes. In finance, AI could automate financial planning and provide personalized investment advice. In retail, AI could personalize shopping experiences and improve customer service.

Preparing for a Future Dominated by AI

As AI continues to evolve, it's crucial to prepare for a future dominated by this technology. Here are a few ways to do so:

1. **Education and Lifelong Learning**: As AI changes the job landscape, it's essential to continually learn and acquire new skills. This could involve learning about AI and related technologies, as well as developing skills that complement AI, such as critical thinking and creativity.

2. **Embrace Change**: As AI transforms various industries, it's important to be open to change. This could involve adopting new technologies, adapting to new ways of working, and being flexible in the face of uncertainty.

3. **Ethical Considerations**: As AI raises ethical issues, it's important to consider these issues and participate in discussions about the ethical use of AI.

In conclusion, the future of AI holds immense possibilities, but also challenges. By understanding these predictions and preparing for the future, we can harness the potential of AI and navigate the challenges it presents. In the next lesson, we will debunk some common myths about AI. Stay tune

"The future is here, it's just not evenly distributed yet." - William Gibson

1.8 Debunking AI Myths

Introduction

In this lesson, we will focus on debunking some of the common myths and misconceptions about Artificial Intelligence (AI). These myths often stem from misunderstandings, over-hype, or fear of the unknown. By addressing these misconceptions, we hope to provide a clearer understanding of what AI is, what it can and cannot do, and its role in our lives and various sectors.

Common Misconceptions About AI

Myth 1: AI is an All-Knowing, All-Powerful Entity

Contrary to popular belief, AI is not an omnipotent or omniscient entity. It is a tool created by humans, and its capabilities are limited to what it has been programmed to do. It learns from data and makes decisions based on that data, but it does not possess consciousness or emotions.

Myth 2: AI Will Replace All Jobs

While AI is indeed reshaping the job market and may replace certain tasks, it is not likely to replace all jobs. Many jobs require human skills such as creativity, empathy, and critical thinking, which AI currently cannot replicate. Instead, AI is expected to create new jobs and change the nature of existing ones.

Myth 3: AI is Only for Tech Giants and Large Corporations

AI is not exclusive to tech giants or large corporations. With the democratization of AI technologies, even small businesses and startups can leverage AI to improve their operations, make data-driven decisions, and provide better services.

The Reality of AI: What It Can and Cannot Do

AI has made significant strides in various fields, from healthcare and finance to education and entertainment. It can analyze vast amounts of data, identify patterns, make predictions, and automate repetitive tasks. However, AI also has its limitations. It lacks the ability to understand context like humans do, it can be biased based on the data it was trained on, and it cannot replicate human creativity or emotional intelligence.

The Importance of Understanding AI Beyond the Hype

Understanding AI beyond the hype is crucial for several reasons. It allows us to make informed decisions about implementing AI in different sectors, it helps us prepare for the changes that AI brings to the job market, and it enables us to address the ethical and privacy concerns associated with AI. By debunking AI myths, we can have a more realistic and balanced view of AI and its potential impact on our lives and society.

Conclusion

In this lesson, we have debunked some common AI myths and shed light on the reality of AI. As we continue to explore the world of AI in this course, remember that understanding AI is not just about grasping its technical aspects, but also about discerning the hype from the reality and recognizing its implications in various sectors.

"AI is not just a tool; it's a mirror reflecting our most complex selves and challenging us to be better."
- Dennis Frank

1.9 Ethical Considerations in AI

Introduction

Artificial Intelligence (AI) is an incredible technological advancement that is transforming our world in numerous ways. However, as with any powerful tool, it comes with its own set of ethical considerations. As we continue to incorporate AI into various aspects of our lives, it's crucial to understand these ethical implications and navigate them effectively.

The Importance of Ethical Considerations

AI is not merely a technological issue; it's a societal one. As AI systems become more integrated into our daily lives, they inevitably affect human values, rights, norms, and behaviors. Therefore, ethical considerations are not just an add-on to AI development; they are a fundamental part of it.

The decisions made by AI systems can have profound impacts on individuals and society. For instance, AI algorithms used in hiring processes could inadvertently discriminate against certain groups of people. Autonomous vehicles must make decisions in scenarios where human life is at stake. AI systems handling sensitive data must do so with respect for privacy and consent.

All these examples highlight why ethical considerations are crucial in the AI revolution. They help us ensure that AI technologies are developed and used in a way that respects human rights, promotes fairness, and benefits society as a whole.

Balancing the Benefits of AI with Ethical Considerations

While AI presents enormous potential benefits, such as improving efficiency, enabling new services, and solving complex problems, we must balance these with ethical considerations. This balancing act is not always straightforward. It requires ongoing dialogue among AI developers, users, ethicists, and policymakers.

One approach to achieving this balance is to incorporate ethical considerations into the design and deployment of AI systems. This could involve using techniques to reduce bias in AI algorithms, implementing transparency measures to make AI decisions understandable to users, and ensuring that AI systems are accountable for their actions.

Another approach is to establish ethical guidelines and regulations for AI. These could set standards for AI behavior, provide mechanisms for addressing ethical issues, and ensure that those who develop and use AI are held accountable for adhering to these standards.

Conclusion

In conclusion, as we continue to embrace the AI revolution, we must not lose sight of the ethical considerations that it raises. By understanding these issues and taking proactive steps to address them, we can ensure that AI serves as a tool for enhancing human wellbeing and upholding our shared values.

In the next lesson, we will conclude this module by discussing how we can embrace the AI revolution while navigating these ethical considerations.

"The pace of progress in artificial intelligence (I'm not referring to narrow AI) is incredibly fast. Unless you have direct exposure to groups like Deep-Mind, you have no idea how fast—it is growing at a pace close to exponential." - Elon Musk

1.10 Conclusion: Embracing the AI Revolution

As we conclude this module, let's take a moment to reflect on the journey we've embarked on. We started with a basic understanding of what AI is and how it works, and gradually explored the various ways it is subtly revolutionizing our world.

Recap of Key Points

We've covered a lot of ground in this module. We began by demystifying AI and breaking down its core concepts and terminologies. We then delved into the different applications of AI in our everyday lives, from our smartphones to our workplaces. We also explored the evolution of AI, tracing its journey from a mere concept to a powerful force that is driving an invisible revolution in various sectors of our society.

Embracing AI

The importance of understanding and embracing AI cannot be overstated. As we've seen, AI is not just a technological trend; it's a paradigm shift that's reshaping the way we live, work, and interact with the world. By understanding AI, we can better appreciate its benefits, mitigate its risks, and harness its potential to solve complex problems and improve our lives.

Looking Ahead: The Future of AI

As we look ahead, the future of AI holds immense possibilities. From autonomous vehicles and smart homes to personalized healthcare and advanced robotics, AI is poised to transform every aspect of our lives. But with these advancements come new challenges and ethical considerations, such as privacy concerns and the risk of job displacement.

It's crucial that we not only keep pace with the AI revolution but also actively participate in shaping its direction. This involves continuous learning, staying informed about the latest developments, and engaging in discussions about the ethical implications of AI.

In the next module, we will delve into how AI is reshaping the job market and the skills required to stay relevant in this AI-driven era.

Remember, the AI revolution is not something that's happening in some distant future; it's happening here and now. And the more we understand and embrace it, the better equipped we will be to thrive in this exciting new era.

So, let's continue this journey together, exploring and demystifying the fascinating world of AI.

2.1 The AI Revolution in the Job Market

Welcome to the first lesson of the second module - "The AI Workforce: Evolving Careers and Skills". In this lesson, we will explore the profound impact of the AI revolution on the job market. We will delve into how AI is not only changing the nature of work but also creating new roles and opportunities.

Understanding the AI Revolution and Its Impact on the Job Market

The AI revolution is not a distant future concept; it's happening right now. As AI technologies continue to evolve and permeate various sectors, they are fundamentally altering the way we work. AI is automating repetitive tasks, enhancing decision-making processes, and providing unprecedented levels of efficiency and accuracy.

However, this AI-driven transformation is not without its challenges. As AI systems take over certain tasks, there is a growing concern about job displacement. While it's true that some roles may become obsolete, it's equally important to note that AI is also creating new jobs that didn't exist before. These roles, often requiring a unique blend of skills, are at the forefront of this AI revolution.

The Shift from Traditional Jobs to AI-Driven Roles

As AI continues to advance, we are witnessing a significant shift in the job market. Traditional roles are being redefined, and entirely new AI-driven roles are emerging. For instance, jobs such as data scientists, AI ethicists, and machine learning engineers are now in high demand.

This shift is not confined to the tech industry alone. From healthcare and finance to retail and entertainment, AI is creating new job categories across various sectors. The key to navigating this shift successfully lies in understanding the changing skills landscape and adapting accordingly.

Case Studies of Industries Already Influenced by AI

Let's take a look at a few industries that are already feeling the impact of AI.

Healthcare: AI is revolutionizing healthcare with roles like AI data analysts who interpret health data to predict and improve patient outcomes. AI is also creating opportunities for AI ethicists who ensure the ethical use of AI in patient care.

Finance: In the finance sector, AI is used for fraud detection, risk assessment, and personalized banking services. This has led to the rise of roles such as AI financial analysts and AI risk officers.

Retail: AI is transforming the retail sector with personalized shopping experiences and efficient supply chain management. This has resulted in new roles like AI retail strategists and AI supply chain analysts.

In conclusion, the AI revolution in the job market is a dynamic, ongoing process. While it presents challenges, it also offers exciting new opportunities. In the next lesson, we will delve deeper into these new careers in AI and explore how they are shaping the future of work.

"In the long term, artificial intelligence and automation are going to be taking over so much of what gives humans a feeling of purpose."
- Matt Bellamy

2.2 The Rise of New Careers in AI

In this lesson, we will delve into the fascinating world of new careers that have emerged as a result of advancements in Artificial Intelligence (AI). We will explore the roles of AI specialists and data scientists and discuss the increasing demand for AI ethicists.

Exploration of New Careers Born Out of AI Advancement

The AI revolution has not only transformed existing jobs but has also given birth to entirely new careers. As AI continues to evolve, we are witnessing the rise of new professions that were unheard of a few years ago. These new careers are born out of the need to develop, manage, and utilize AI technologies effectively.

Some of the new careers that have emerged include AI specialists, data scientists, machine learning engineers, AI ethicists, and AI project managers, among others. These professionals play a crucial role in harnessing the power of AI, ensuring it is used responsibly, and driving innovation in various sectors.

The Role of AI Specialists and Data Scientists

AI Specialists and Data Scientists are at the forefront of the AI revolution.

AI Specialists are responsible for designing and implementing AI systems. They work closely with other professionals to understand their needs and develop AI solutions that can help meet these needs. AI Specialists need a strong understanding of AI technologies, programming skills, and the ability to think creatively and solve complex problems.

Data Scientists, on the other hand, play a crucial role in making sense of the vast amounts of data that AI systems generate. They use statistical techniques and machine learning algorithms to analyze and interpret complex data sets. They help organizations make data-driven decisions, identify trends, and predict future outcomes.

The Increasing Demand for AI Ethicists

As AI continues to permeate various aspects of our lives, ethical considerations have come to the forefront. This has led to the emergence of a new profession - the AI Ethicist.

AI Ethicists are responsible for ensuring that AI technologies are developed and used in an ethical manner. They consider the moral implications of AI, such as privacy concerns, bias in AI algorithms, and the impact of AI on jobs and society. They work with organizations to develop ethical guidelines for AI use and advocate for responsible AI practices.

The demand for AI Ethicists is on the rise as more organizations recognize the importance of ethical considerations in AI development and use. This trend underscores the need for a multi-disciplinary approach to AI, where technical skills are complemented by a strong understanding of ethical principles.

In conclusion, the rise of AI has ushered in a new era of careers. As we continue to navigate the AI revolution, these new professions will play a crucial role in shaping the future of AI and ensuring it brings about positive change in our world.

In the next lesson, we will explore how AI is impacting traditional professions.

"The rise of powerful AI will be either the best thing, or the worst, ever to happen to humanity. We do not yet know which." - Stephen Hawking

2.3 AI's Impact on Traditional Professions

Artificial Intelligence (AI) is not just creating new career opportunities, but also transforming traditional professions. This shift is particularly noticeable in sectors like law, medicine, and finance, where AI's ability to analyze vast amounts of data and automate routine tasks is proving to be a game-changer.

Transforming Traditional Professions

Law

In the field of law, AI is being utilized to automate tasks such as legal research, contract analysis, and document review. AI-powered legal tools can sift through hundreds of legal cases, statutes, and regulations in a fraction of the time it would take a human lawyer. This not only increases efficiency but also reduces the risk of human error.

Medicine

In medicine, AI is revolutionizing diagnosis, treatment planning, and patient care. AI algorithms can analyze medical images, detect anomalies, and even predict patient risk for certain diseases. This allows healthcare professionals to make more accurate diagnoses and provide personalized treatment plans.

Finance

In finance, AI is transforming everything from personal finance management to investment strategies. AI-powered tools can analyze market trends, make predictions, and provide personalized financial advice. This allows financial professionals to make more informed decisions and offer better services to their clients.

The Shift from Manual to AI-Assisted Tasks

The rise of AI in these traditional professions doesn't necessarily mean that humans will be replaced. Instead, professionals are now working alongside AI, using it as a tool to enhance their work. This shift from manual to AI-assisted tasks allows professionals to focus on more complex and strategic aspects of their work, while AI handles the more routine and data-intensive tasks.

Adapting to AI Changes in Traditional Career Paths

As AI continues to reshape traditional professions, it's crucial for professionals to adapt to these changes. This might involve learning new skills, such as data analysis or machine learning, or redefining their roles to focus on tasks that require human skills like critical thinking, creativity, and empathy.

Embracing AI can open up new opportunities for professionals, allowing them to provide better services, make more informed decisions, and ultimately, enhance their career prospects in the AI-driven future.

In the next lesson, we will delve deeper into the skills needed to thrive in an AI-driven job market.

2.4 Skills Needed to Thrive in an AI-Driven Job Market

In this lesson, we will delve into the key skills necessary to thrive in an evolving job market heavily influenced by Artificial Intelligence (AI). As AI continues to permeate various industries, the demand for certain skills, both technical and soft, is on the rise. We will explore these skills and discuss why they are crucial in an AI-dominated world.

Technical Skills

Programming and Data Analysis

In the realm of AI, technical skills, particularly programming and data analysis, are indispensable. Programming skills, especially in languages such as Python, R, and Java, are fundamental to developing and implementing AI algorithms. Similarly, data analysis skills are crucial as AI heavily relies on data to learn and make predictions. Understanding how to collect, clean, analyze, and interpret data is a vital skill in the AI-driven job market.

Soft Skills

While technical skills are essential, soft skills are equally important in the AI-dominated world. Here are two key soft skills that are highly valued:

Critical Thinking

AI systems are designed to make decisions based on data, but they lack the human ability to think critically. As such, individuals who can critically evaluate AI outputs, question assumptions, and make context-based decisions will be highly sought after.

Creativity

AI can generate solutions based on data, but it cannot replicate human creativity. The ability to think outside the box, innovate, and come up with unique solutions is a valuable skill in the AI-driven job market. Creativity will be key in designing novel AI applications and finding new ways to leverage AI in various fields.

Continuous Learning and Adaptation

The world of AI is dynamic and rapidly evolving. As such, the ability to continuously learn and adapt is crucial. This includes staying updated with the latest AI trends, learning new tools and technologies, and being able to adapt to changing job roles and responsibilities. Lifelong learning is no longer an option but a necessity in the AI era.

In conclusion, to thrive in the AI-driven job market, one needs a blend of technical skills, soft skills, and the ability to continuously learn and adapt. As AI continues to revolutionize the job market, these skills will become increasingly important, and individuals who possess them will be well-positioned to seize the opportunities that AI brings.

In the next lesson, we will explore how to prepare for AI-driven careers through education and training.

2.5 Preparing for AI-Driven Careers: Education and Training

In this lesson, we delve into the vital role of education and training in preparing individuals for AI-driven careers. We'll explore the emergence of AI-specific courses and degrees and discuss the importance of lifelong learning and up-skilling in the AI era.

The Role of Education in Preparing for AI-Driven Careers

In the AI-driven job market, education plays a crucial role in equipping individuals with the necessary skills and knowledge. It's not just about understanding AI concepts but also about learning how to apply these concepts in real-world scenarios. Schools, colleges, and universities worldwide are recognizing this need and are increasingly incorporating AI-related subjects into their curriculums.

Emergence of AI-Specific Courses and Degrees

To cater to the growing demand for AI expertise, numerous institutions now offer AI-specific courses and degrees. These range from short-term certificate courses to comprehensive degree programs. These programs are designed to provide in-depth knowledge about AI, machine learning, deep learning, neural networks, and other related fields. They also focus on practical aspects, allowing students to work on projects and case studies that simulate real-world AI applications.

The Importance of Lifelong Learning and Upskilling in the AI Era

In the rapidly evolving field of AI, it's not enough to rely solely on formal education. Lifelong learning and continuous upskilling have become essential. Professionals need to stay updated with the latest advancements and trends in AI. This can be achieved through online courses, webinars, work-shops, and reading relevant literature.

Moreover, soft skills like problem-solving, critical thinking, and creativity are equally important in the AI era. AI systems can perform routine tasks and analyze data, but human crea-tivity and critical thinking are crucial for designing innovative solutions and making strategic decisions.

Conclusion

Preparing for AI-driven careers requires a blend of formal education, continuous learning, and the development of soft skills. As AI continues to evolve and reshape various indus-tries, individuals who can adapt and continuously upgrade their skills will be the ones who thrive in the AI-driven job market.

In the next lesson, we'll explore the future of work in the AI era, focusing on the opportunities and challenges that AI brings to the job market.

2.6 AI and the Future of Work: Opportunities and Challenges

In this lesson, we will delve into the potential opportunities and challenges that AI presents to the job market. We'll also discuss strategies for navigating the AI revolution in the job market. Let's get started!

The Opportunities Presented by AI in the Job Market

Artificial Intelligence (AI) is a powerful tool that has the potential to revolutionize the job market. Here are some of the opportunities it presents:

1. **Creation of New Jobs**: AI can lead to the creation of new jobs that didn't exist before. These include roles like AI specialists, data scientists, and machine learning engineers.

2. **Increased Productivity**: AI can automate repetitive tasks, freeing up time for workers to focus on more complex and creative tasks. This can lead to increased productivity and job satisfaction.

3. **Improved Decision Making**: AI can analyze vast amounts of data quickly and accurately, helping businesses make better decisions. This can lead to improved business performance and competitiveness.

The Challenges and Risks Associated with an AI-Driven Workforce

While AI presents numerous opportunities, it also comes with its own set of challenges and risks:

1. **Job Displacement**: There's a fear that AI could replace certain jobs, leading to job displacement. This is especially a concern for roles that involve routine tasks.

2. **Skills Gap**: The rise of AI is creating a demand for new skills. However, there's a gap between the skills workers currently have and the skills needed for AI-driven jobs.

3. **Ethical and Privacy Concerns**: AI systems often need large amounts of data to function effectively. This raises concerns about data privacy and ethical use of AI.

Strategies for Navigating the AI Revolution in the Job Market

Given these opportunities and challenges, here are some strategies for navigating the AI revolution in the job market:

1. **Lifelong Learning**: To stay relevant in an AI-driven job market, it's important to embrace lifelong learning. This includes learning about AI and related technologies.

2. **Adaptability**: As AI continues to evolve, it's crucial to be adaptable. This means being open to new ways of working and being willing to acquire new skills.

3. **Ethical Awareness**: Given the ethical and privacy concerns associated with AI, it's important to be aware of these issues and how to navigate them.

In conclusion, AI presents both opportunities and challenges to the job market. By understanding these and adopting the right strategies, you can navigate the AI revolution and thrive in an AI-driven job market.

In the next lesson, we will explore real-life case studies of AI in the tech and healthcare industries.

"Technology is a useful servant but a dangerous master."
- Christian Lous Lange

2.7 Case Study: AI in the Tech Industry

In this lesson, we will take a deep dive into the tech industry, one of the sectors at the forefront of the AI revolution. We will explore how AI is reshaping jobs, how it's shifting the paradigm from traditional software development to AI-driven development, and the role of AI in tech entrepreneurship.

An In-depth Look at How AI is Reshaping Jobs in the Tech Industry

The tech industry has always been a rapidly evolving field. However, the advent of AI has accelerated this evolution to an unprecedented pace. AI is not just another technology; it's a transformative force that is redefining roles and creating entirely new jobs in the tech industry.

AI specialists, data scientists, machine learning engineers, and robotics experts are now in high demand. These roles require a deep understanding of AI algorithms and the ability to apply them in real-world scenarios. However, it's not just about creating AI; it's also about understanding how to integrate AI with existing systems, manage AI projects, and navigate the ethical and legal implications of AI. This has led to the emergence of roles like AI ethicists and AI project managers.

The Shift from Traditional Software Development to AI-Driven Development

Traditional software development is deterministic, with developers writing explicit instructions for the software to follow. However, AI-driven development is probabilistic. Instead of writing explicit instructions, developers create models that learn from data and make predictions or decisions based on that learning.

This shift has profound implications for software development. It requires a new set of skills, including data science, machine learning, and statistics. It also changes the software development lifecycle. AI models need to be trained, validated, and continuously updated as new data becomes available. This has led to the rise of MLOps, a practice that combines machine learning, DevOps, and data engineering to manage the lifecycle of AI models.

The Role of AI in Tech Entrepreneurship

AI is also creating opportunities for tech entrepreneurs. It's enabling startups to create innovative products and services that were previously unimaginable. From AI-powered chatbots that provide customer service to AI-driven analytics platforms that provide insights from big data, the possibilities are endless.

However, leveraging AI is not without its challenges. Tech entrepreneurs need to navigate issues like data privacy, algorithmic bias, and the black box problem, where AI decisions are not easily explainable. They also need to build multidisciplinary teams that can bridge the gap between AI technology and business applications.

In conclusion, AI is transforming the tech industry in profound ways. It's reshaping jobs, changing the way software is developed, and creating new opportunities for tech entre-preneurs. As we move further into the AI era, these trends are likely to intensify, making it essential for tech professionals to understand and adapt to the AI revolution.

In the next lesson, we will explore another case study: AI in the healthcare industry. We will delve into how AI is revolu-tionizing diagnosis, treatment planning, patient care, and more.

"Technology is the knack of so ar-ranging the world that we don't have to experience it." - Max Frisch

2.8 Case Study - AI in the Healthcare Industry

In this lesson, we will delve into a case study that explores the impact of Artificial Intelligence (AI) on the healthcare industry. We will examine how AI is reshaping jobs in this sector, the emergence of new roles driven by AI, and what the future holds for healthcare professions in the age of AI.

Understanding the Impact of AI on Jobs in the Healthcare Industry

AI has been a game-changer in the healthcare industry, transforming various aspects from diagnosis to treatment, patient care, and administrative tasks. With AI's ability to analyze vast amounts of data, make predictions, and automate repetitive tasks, it's not surprising that it's reshaping jobs in the healthcare sector.

For instance, radiologists, who traditionally spend hours analyzing images, can now use AI-powered tools to detect anomalies with greater speed and accuracy. This doesn't mean that radiologists will be replaced by AI. Instead, their role is evolving to become more focused on complex cases and patient care, while AI takes care of routine image analysis.

Similarly, AI is also automating administrative tasks such as scheduling appointments, maintaining patient records, and billing. This allows healthcare administrators to focus on more strategic tasks and patient interaction.

The Emergence of AI-Driven Roles in the Healthcare Industry

As AI continues to permeate the healthcare industry, new roles are emerging that are centered around the effective use of AI. Let's look at a couple of these roles:

- **Healthcare Data Analysts**: These professionals are responsible for managing and interpreting the vast amounts of data generated in healthcare settings. They use AI tools to analyze this data and provide insights that can improve patient care, streamline operations, and inform policy decisions.

- **AI Ethicists**: With the increasing use of AI in healthcare, there's a growing need for professionals who can navigate the ethical implications of AI. AI ethicists in healthcare work to ensure that AI applications respect patient privacy, provide equitable care, and are transparent in their operations.

The Future of Healthcare Professions in the Age of AI

The future of healthcare professions in the age of AI looks promising. As AI takes over routine tasks, healthcare professionals can focus more on patient care and complex cases that require human judgment. Additionally, the emergence of new roles provides exciting opportunities for professionals to specialize in AI-related fields.

However, this transition also requires healthcare professionals to upskill and adapt to the changing landscape. Skills in data analysis, understanding of AI tools, and ethical decision-making will be increasingly important in the healthcare industry.

In conclusion, AI is not replacing jobs in the healthcare industry; it's transforming them. By embracing AI, healthcare professionals can not only enhance their careers but also contribute to a healthcare system that's more efficient, effective, and patient-centered.

In the next lesson, we will explore another case study that delves into the impact of AI on the tech industry.

"The real problem is not whether machines think but whether men do."
- B.F. Skinner

2.9 Navigating Career Transitions in the AI Era

In this lesson, we will delve into the importance of navigating career transitions in the AI era. We will also discuss strategies for successful career transitions in an AI-driven job market and explore case studies of successful career transitions in the AI era.

Understanding the Need for Career Transitions in the AI Era

The advent of AI has significantly transformed the job market. Traditional roles are being reshaped, and new careers are emerging. This evolution necessitates a shift in our career paths to stay relevant.

AI is not just creating new jobs; it is also altering existing ones. For instance, data analysts now need to be familiar with AI-powered data analysis tools. Similarly, marketers need to understand how AI can enhance customer segmentation and targeting. Therefore, even if your job isn't directly related to AI, it's likely that AI will affect how you work.

Strategies for Successful Career Transitions in an AI-Driven Job Market

Navigating career transitions in the AI era can be challenging, but with the right strategies, you can successfully adapt to the changing job market. Here are some strategies to consider:

1. Lifelong Learning: Embrace the concept of lifelong learning. Keep abreast of the latest developments in AI and related fields. Online courses, workshops, and seminars can be excellent resources.

2. Skill Development: Identify the skills that are in demand in the AI era and work on developing them. These could include technical skills like programming and data analysis, as well as soft skills like problem-solving and critical thinking.

3. Networking: Connect with professionals in the AI field. Networking can provide insights into industry trends and potential job opportunities.

4. Career Counseling: Consider seeking advice from career counselors who specialize in AI-related careers. They can provide personalized guidance based on your skills, interests, and career goals.

Case Studies of Successful Career Transitions in the AI Era

To illustrate how these strategies can be applied, let's look at a couple of case studies of successful career transitions in the AI era.

Case Study 1: The Data Analyst Turned AI Specialist

John was a data analyst with a background in statistics. When his company started using AI-powered data analysis tools, he saw an opportunity to enhance his career. He took online courses in AI and machine learning and started applying these concepts at work. His proactive approach helped him transition into a new role as an AI specialist in his company.

Case Study 2: The Marketer Turned AI Strategist

Sarah was a marketer with a knack for understanding customer behavior. When her company started using AI for customer segmentation, she realized that she needed to understand AI to stay relevant. She took courses in AI for marketing and started incorporating AI strategies into her work. This led to her transitioning into a new role as an AI strategist in her company.

In conclusion, navigating career transitions in the AI era requires a proactive approach, a commitment to learning, and the ability to adapt to new technologies. By understanding the impact of AI on your field and taking steps to develop relevant skills, you can successfully transition your career in the AI era.

2.10 The AI Workforce: Looking Ahead

In this lesson, we will delve into the future of the AI work-force. We will explore the predicted trends in the AI job market, understand the role of AI in shaping the future of work, and discuss how to stay relevant in the AI era.

Predicting Future Trends in the AI Job Market

The AI job market is poised for significant growth in the coming years. According to the World Economic Forum, by 2025, machines will perform more current work tasks than humans. It's estimated that 85 million jobs may be displaced by a shift in the division of labor between humans and machines, while 97 million new roles may emerge that are more adapted to the new division of labor between humans, machines, and algorithms.

AI and machine learning specialists are among the roles that are expected to be in high demand. Other roles that are likely to see growth include data analysts and scientists, big data specialists, process automation experts, information security analysts, and digital transformation specialists.

The Role of AI in Shaping the Future of Work

AI is not just creating new jobs; it's also transforming the way we work. Automation is taking over routine tasks, freeing up humans to focus on more complex and creative tasks. AI is also enabling remote work and flexible working arrangements, which are becoming increasingly popular.

Furthermore, AI is expected to play a significant role in decision-making processes, with predictive analytics and data-driven insights guiding strategic decisions. AI can also enhance collaboration and productivity by streamlining workflows and communication processes.

Preparing for the Future: Staying Relevant in the AI Era

In the face of these changes, it's crucial to stay relevant and competitive. Here are a few strategies:

Continuous Learning: As AI continues to evolve, so too should our knowledge and skills. Engage in lifelong learning, continually updating your skills to stay abreast of the latest developments in AI.

Adaptability: Be open to change and ready to adapt. This includes being willing to switch roles or industries and being comfortable with new ways of working, such as remote work or flexible hours.

Soft Skills: While technical skills are important, soft skills like critical thinking, creativity, and emotional intelligence will be increasingly valuable as AI takes over more routine tasks.

Ethics and AI: As AI becomes more prevalent, understanding the ethical implications of AI will be increasingly important. This includes understanding issues around privacy, bias, and fairness in AI.

In conclusion, the future of the AI workforce is bright, full of opportunities for those who are prepared to adapt and evolve. By staying informed, being adaptable, and focusing on both technical and soft skills, you can thrive in the AI era.

"The human spirit must prevail over technology." - Albert Einstein

3.1 Introduction to AI in Personal Finance and Retail

Welcome to the first lesson of our third module, "Money and Machines: AI in Personal Finance and Retail". In this lesson, we will explore the fascinating intersection of artificial intelligence (AI) with personal finance and retail sectors. We will understand how AI is transforming these sectors and what it means for consumers and businesses.

Understanding the Role of AI in Personal Finance and Retail

Artificial intelligence, with its ability to analyze vast amounts of data and make predictions, is revolutionizing personal finance and retail sectors. In personal finance, AI is being used in various ways, from robo-advisors that provide investment advice to chatbots that help with budgeting. Similarly, in the retail sector, AI is being used to personalize shopping experiences, manage inventory, and even predict future trends.

The Transformation Brought About by AI in These Sectors

AI is bringing about a significant transformation in both personal finance and retail sectors. In personal finance, AI is making financial advice accessible to more people, automating tedious tasks, and providing more accurate predictions.

This is leading to more efficient financial management and better financial outcomes for individuals.

In the retail sector, AI is enhancing customer experiences by providing personalized recommendations, improving inventory management, and reducing operational costs. This is leading to increased customer satisfaction, higher sales, and improved profitability for retail businesses.

The Implications of AI for Consumers and Businesses

The implications of AI in personal finance and retail are profound. For consumers, AI is making financial management easier and more efficient. It's also making shopping more personalized and convenient. For businesses, AI is providing a competitive edge by improving efficiency and customer satisfaction. However, it's also presenting new challenges, such as the need for data privacy and the risk of job displacement due to automation.

In the next lessons, we will delve deeper into these topics and explore how AI is reshaping personal finance and retail, the benefits it offers, and the challenges it presents. We will also look at some case studies to understand the practical applications of AI in these sectors.

Remember, as we journey through this module, the goal is not just to understand the concepts but also to think critically about the implications of AI and how we can adapt to this rapidly changing landscape. So, let's embark on this exciting journey and uncover the world of AI in personal finance and retail!

3.2 AI and Personal Finance: A New Era

Introduction

In this lesson, we will explore the transformative role of Artificial Intelligence (AI) in personal finance management. As AI continues to evolve, it is reshaping the financial landscape, making it more accessible, efficient, and personalized. Whether it's budgeting, investing, or financial planning, AI is becoming an indispensable tool in managing our finances.

The Role of AI in Personal Finance Management

Artificial Intelligence has revolutionized personal finance management by automating complex tasks, providing personalized recommendations, and enhancing decision-making processes. It has made financial services more accessible to a wider audience, democratizing access to financial advice that was once available only to the affluent.

AI-driven platforms can analyze vast amounts of financial data in real time, providing insights and recommendations tailored to individual financial goals and risk tolerance. This allows users to make more informed decisions about their finances, helping them achieve their financial goals more efficiently.

AI in Budgeting

Budgeting is a fundamental aspect of personal finance management. AI has made budgeting more intuitive and user-friendly, with apps that can track spending, categorize transactions, and provide real-time insights into spending habits.

For instance, AI can analyze your spending patterns and identify areas where you could potentially save money. It can also set up budgets based on your income and expenses, and alert you when you're nearing your spending limit. This makes budgeting less of a chore and more of a seamless part of daily life.

AI in Investing

Investing is another area where AI has made significant strides. Robo-advisors, powered by AI algorithms, have democratized investing by making it more accessible and affordable. These platforms can create personalized investment portfolios based on your financial goals and risk tolerance, and automatically rebalance your portfolio as needed.

AI can also analyze vast amounts of market data to predict market trends and provide investment recommendations. This can help investors make more informed decisions and potentially increase their returns.

AI in Financial Planning

Financial planning involves setting financial goals and developing a plan to achieve them. AI can simplify this process by providing personalized financial advice based on your income, expenses, financial goals, and risk tolerance.

For instance, AI can help you plan for retirement by estimating how much you need to save and recommending a savings plan. It can also help you plan for major life events, like buying a house or starting a family, by providing financial projections and advice.

Case Studies of AI Applications in Personal Finance

Let's look at some real-world examples of how AI is transforming personal finance:

1. **Mint**: This budgeting app uses AI to track and categorize transactions, create budgets, and provide insights into spending habits. It can also provide personalized tips to help users save money.

2. **Betterment**: This robo-advisor uses AI to create personalized investment portfolios based on users' financial goals and risk tolerance. It also automatically rebalances portfolios as needed.

3. **Credit Karma**: This platform uses AI to provide personalized credit and loan recommendations based on users' credit scores and financial goals.

These examples illustrate how AI is making personal finance management more accessible, efficient, and personalized.

Conclusion

Artificial Intelligence is ushering in a new era in personal finance management. By automating complex tasks, providing personalized recommendations, and enhancing decision-making processes, AI is making personal finance more accessible and user-friendly. As we continue to embrace AI in our daily lives, we can expect it to play an even more significant role in managing our finances in the future.

3.3 AI in Retail: Revolutionizing Shopping Experiences

In this lesson, we will explore how Artificial Intelligence (AI) is transforming the retail industry, making it smarter, more efficient, and more customer-centric. We will delve into the use of AI in inventory management, customer service, and personalized marketing, and we will also look at some real-world case studies of AI applications in retail.

Understanding How AI is Transforming the Retail Industry

The retail industry is one of the sectors that have been significantly impacted by AI. With the advent of AI, retailers can now analyze vast amounts of data to gain insights into customer behavior, manage inventory more efficiently, and provide personalized shopping experiences. AI is helping retailers to predict trends, understand customer preferences, and make informed decisions, thereby revolutionizing the retail industry.

The Use of AI in Inventory Management

AI is playing a crucial role in inventory management in the retail industry. With AI, retailers can predict demand for products, optimize stock levels, and reduce waste. AI algorithms analyze historical sales data, current market trends, and other relevant factors to forecast demand accurately. This helps retailers to maintain optimal inventory levels, reducing the risk of stockouts or overstocking, and thus saving costs.

The Use of AI in Customer Service

AI is also transforming customer service in retail. Many retailers are now using AI-powered chatbots to handle customer inquiries, complaints, and requests. These chatbots can provide instant responses, handle multiple queries simultaneously, and operate 24/7, thus improving customer service efficiency and customer satisfaction. AI is also used in virtual assistants that guide customers through the shopping process, making product recommendations based on customer preferences and past purchases.

The Use of AI in Personalized Marketing

Personalized marketing is another area where AI is making a significant impact. AI algorithms can analyze customer data to understand individual preferences, shopping habits, and buying behavior. This enables retailers to create personalized marketing campaigns that target individual customers with products and offers that are likely to interest them. This not only improves customer engagement and loyalty but also boosts sales and profitability.

Case Studies of AI Applications in Retail

Let's look at some real-world examples of how AI is being used in the retail industry:

1. **Amazon**: Amazon uses AI for a variety of purposes, including personalized recommendations, customer service, and inventory management. Amazon's recommendation engine uses AI to analyze customer data and suggest products that customers might like based on their past purchases and browsing history.

2. **Walmart**: Walmart uses AI to manage its inventory and supply chain. The company uses AI algorithms to analyze sales data and predict demand for products, helping it to maintain optimal inventory levels and reduce waste.

3. **Starbucks**: Starbucks uses AI to provide personalized marketing to its customers. The company's AI-powered system analyzes customer data to understand individual preferences and habits, and then sends personalized offers and recommendations to customers.

In conclusion, AI is revolutionizing the retail industry, making it more efficient, customer-centric, and profitable. As AI technology continues to evolve, we can expect to see even more innovative applications of AI in retail in the future.

In the next lesson, we will explore the benefits of AI in personal finance and retail.

3.4 The Benefits of AI in Personal Finance and Retail

Artificial Intelligence has become a game-changer in both personal finance and retail sectors. It offers a myriad of benefits that are transforming the way consumers manage their finances and shopping experiences. In this lesson, we'll delve into the advantages of using AI for consumers and businesses, how it can lead to improved financial decisions and shopping experiences, and the potential for AI to drive growth and efficiency in these sectors.

Advantages of AI for Consumers and Businesses

AI presents numerous advantages for both consumers and businesses. For consumers, AI-powered tools can help manage finances more effectively, offering personalized financial advice, budgeting assistance, and automated investments. These tools can analyze vast amounts of data to provide insights that help consumers make informed financial decisions.

On the other hand, businesses can leverage AI to analyze consumer behavior, predict market trends, and automate routine tasks. This leads to increased efficiency, reduced operational costs, and improved customer service.

Improved Financial Decisions and Shopping Experiences

AI has the potential to revolutionize financial decision-making and shopping experiences. AI-powered financial advisors, also known as robo-advisors, use complex algorithms to analyze market trends and offer personalized investment advice. This can lead to more informed and potentially profitable investment decisions.

In the retail sector, AI can personalize the shopping experience by analyzing customer preferences and behavior to recommend products that are most likely to appeal to the individual shopper. This not only improves the shopping experience but also increases customer satisfaction and loyalty.

Driving Growth and Efficiency

AI holds immense potential to drive growth and efficiency in the personal finance and retail sectors. By automating routine tasks, AI can free up time for businesses to focus on strategic planning and innovation.

In personal finance, AI can automate investment management, reducing the need for human intervention and minimizing errors. This leads to more efficient operations and potentially higher returns on investment.

In retail, AI can streamline inventory management, predict sales trends, and optimize pricing strategies. These capabilities can increase operational efficiency, drive sales growth, and boost profitability.

In conclusion, AI is a powerful tool that offers numerous benefits in personal finance and retail. By improving decision-making, enhancing customer experiences, and driving growth and efficiency, AI is set to revolutionize these sectors.

As we move forward in the AI era, embracing these technologies will become increasingly important for both consumers and businesses. In the next lesson, we'll explore the challenges and risks of AI in personal finance and retail.

"Just because something doesn't do what you planned it to do doesn't mean it's useless." - Thomas Edison

3.5 The Challenges and Risks of AI in Personal Finance and Retail

While artificial intelligence (AI) brings a plethora of benefits to the personal finance and retail sectors, it's essential to acknowledge the challenges and risks associated with its use. In this lesson, we will delve into the potential drawbacks, privacy and security concerns, and the importance of ethical considerations in AI applications in these sectors.

Potential Drawbacks and Risks

AI is a powerful tool that can streamline operations, enhance customer experience, and drive growth in personal finance and retail. However, it's not without its drawbacks and risks.

One of the primary concerns is the potential for job displacement. As AI systems become more capable, there's a risk that they could replace human workers, particularly in roles that involve repetitive tasks or data analysis. This could lead to job losses and require significant workforce retraining.

Another risk is the over-reliance on AI systems. If these systems fail or make mistakes, it could have serious consequences, particularly in the personal finance sector where decisions can have significant financial implications.

Privacy and Security Concerns

AI systems often rely on large amounts of data to function effectively. This can raise privacy and security concerns, particularly when dealing with sensitive financial information.

AI systems can be vulnerable to cyber-attacks, and there's a risk that data could be stolen or misused. Additionally, the use of AI in personal finance and retail could lead to increased surveillance and a loss of privacy.

Ethical Considerations

Ethical considerations are paramount when using AI in any sector, and personal finance and retail are no exceptions.

AI systems need to be designed and used in a way that respects individual rights and freedoms. This includes ensuring that AI systems are transparent, accountable, and do not discriminate.

In the personal finance sector, there's a risk that AI systems could make decisions that unfairly disadvantage certain groups. For example, an AI system might deny a loan application based on factors that are discriminatory.

In the retail sector, there's a risk that AI could be used to manipulate consumers, such as by using personal data to target individuals with specific marketing messages.

Conclusion

While AI holds great promise for the personal finance and retail sectors, it's crucial to be aware of the challenges and risks. By addressing these issues head-on, we can ensure that AI is used in a way that benefits everyone and minimizes potential harm.

In the next lesson, we'll explore the future of AI in personal finance and retail, looking at how these sectors might evolve as AI becomes increasingly integrated into our lives.

"In the symphony of AI, each algorithm is a note, playing its part in harmonizing the future."
- Dennis Frank

.

3.6 The Future of AI in Personal Finance and Retail

In this lesson, we will explore the future trends of AI applications in personal finance and retail. We will also discuss the potential impact of these trends on consumers and businesses and how to prepare for an AI-driven future in these sectors.

Predicting Future Trends in AI Applications in Personal Finance and Retail

Artificial Intelligence is poised to revolutionize personal finance and retail in ways we can only begin to imagine. Here are a few trends to watch out for:

1. **Personalized Financial Advice**: AI-powered robo-advisors will become even more sophisticated, offering personalized financial advice based on individual's financial goals, risk tolerance, and investment preferences.

2. **Automated Budgeting and Saving**: AI will enable more advanced budgeting tools that can predict spending patterns, suggest savings strategies, and even automate savings.

3. **AI-Driven Retail Experiences**: In the retail sector, AI will be used to create highly personalized shopping experiences. This could include AI-powered recommendation systems, virtual shopping assistants, and smart fitting rooms.

4. **Supply Chain Optimization**: AI will be used to streamline supply chains, predict demand, and optimize inventory management, reducing costs and improving efficiency.

The Potential Impact of These Trends on Consumers and Businesses

The potential impact of these trends on consumers and businesses is profound. Here's how:

1. **Empowered Consumers**: AI will empower consumers with personalized financial advice and retail experiences, enabling them to make more informed decisions and get more value for their money.

2. **Efficient Businesses**: Businesses will benefit from AI's ability to streamline operations, optimize supply chains, and personalize customer experiences, leading to increased efficiency and profitability.

3. **Job Market Shift**: As AI automates more tasks in personal finance and retail, there will be a shift in the job market. While some jobs may become obsolete, new roles will emerge that require skills in AI and data analysis.

Preparing for an AI-Driven Future in Personal Finance and Retail

Preparing for an AI-driven future in personal finance and retail involves staying informed about the latest AI trends, investing in AI education and training, and embracing AI as a tool for personal and business growth. Here are some ways to prepare:

1. **Stay Informed**: Keep up with the latest AI trends and developments in personal finance and retail. This could involve reading industry reports, attending webinars, or following thought leaders in the field.

2. **Invest in Education and Training**: Acquire the skills needed to thrive in an AI-driven job market. This could involve taking courses in AI, data analysis, or machine learning.

3. **Embrace AI**: Whether you're a consumer or a business, embrace AI as a tool for growth. This could involve using AI-powered financial tools or integrating AI into your business operations.

In conclusion, the future of AI in personal finance and retail is exciting and full of potential. By staying informed, investing in education and training, and embracing AI, we can prepare for this future and make the most of the opportunities it presents.

3.7 Case Study: AI in Banking

In this lesson, we will explore how Artificial Intelligence (AI) is transforming the banking sector. We will look at the benefits and challenges of AI in banking and draw lessons from its applications in this industry.

AI Transforming the Banking Sector

AI has become a game-changer in the banking sector, revolutionizing the way banking services are delivered and consumed. Banks are leveraging AI to automate routine tasks, enhance customer service, detect fraud, and make data-driven decisions.

For instance, AI-powered chatbots are being used to handle customer inquiries round the clock, providing instant responses and freeing up human resources for more complex tasks. AI algorithms are also being used to analyze vast amounts of data to detect fraudulent transactions, thereby enhancing the security of banking operations.

Moreover, AI is enabling personalized banking by analyzing customer behavior and preferences to offer tailored financial products and services. This not only improves customer satisfaction but also opens new revenue streams for banks.

Benefits and Challenges of AI in Banking

The use of AI in banking comes with several benefits. It improves operational efficiency by automating routine tasks, thus reducing costs and increasing productivity. AI enhances customer service by providing personalized experiences and instant responses to inquiries. It also strengthens security by detecting and preventing fraudulent activities.

However, the adoption of AI in banking is not without challenges. One of the key concerns is data privacy, as AI systems require access to sensitive customer data to function effectively. There's also the risk of AI systems making errors or being manipulated by malicious actors, which could have serious repercussions.

Furthermore, the use of AI could lead to job displacement, as automation may render certain roles redundant. Banks need to manage this transition carefully to avoid social and economic disruptions.

Lessons from AI Applications in Banking

The use of AI in banking provides valuable lessons for other sectors. Firstly, it shows the importance of data in driving AI applications. Banks that have been successful in leveraging AI have done so by harnessing their data effectively.

Secondly, it underscores the need for robust security and privacy measures when dealing with sensitive data. Banks have had to invest heavily in data protection to gain customer trust and comply with regulations.

Finally, it highlights the need for organizations to manage the transition to AI carefully, ensuring that employees are reskilled and redeployed rather than simply replaced.

In conclusion, AI is transforming the banking sector, offering numerous benefits but also posing significant challenges. As we continue to navigate the AI landscape, the lessons drawn from its application in banking will be crucial in shaping its future trajectory.

"Technology is a word that describes something that doesn't work yet."
- Douglas Adams

3.8 Case Study: AI in E-commerce

Understanding how AI is revolutionizing the e-commerce industry

Artificial Intelligence (AI) has been a game-changer for the e-commerce industry. It has enabled businesses to personalize the shopping experience, streamline operations, and improve customer service. AI is used in various aspects of e-commerce, from product recommendations to predictive pricing, customer service bots, and automated warehousing.

AI-powered product recommendations use machine learning algorithms to analyze a customer's browsing and purchasing history, along with data from similar customers, to suggest products that the customer might be interested in. This has been a significant factor in increasing sales and customer satisfaction in e-commerce.

Predictive pricing uses AI to analyze market trends, demand, and competitor pricing to dynamically adjust prices. This maximizes profit and ensures competitiveness.

AI-powered customer service bots, or chatbots, provide instant customer service, answering common queries, and guiding customers through the purchasing process. They can operate 24/7, increasing customer satisfaction and reducing the need for human customer service agents.

Automated warehousing uses AI to manage inventory, predict demand, and optimize the storage and retrieval of products. This reduces costs and increases efficiency.

The benefits and challenges of AI in e-commerce

The benefits of AI in e-commerce are numerous. It allows businesses to provide a personalized shopping experience, increasing customer satisfaction and sales. It improves efficiency and reduces costs in operations and customer service. It also provides valuable insights into customer behavior and market trends, aiding strategic decision-making.

However, there are also challenges. Implementing AI requires significant investment in technology and skills. There are also privacy concerns, as AI relies on analyzing customer data. Businesses must ensure they comply with data protection regulations and maintain customer trust.

Lessons learned from AI applications in e-commerce

AI has proven to be a valuable tool in e-commerce, but it's not a magic solution. Successful implementation requires a clear understanding of the business's needs and the capabilities of AI. It also requires careful management of customer data to maintain trust and comply with regulations.

AI is not a replacement for human staff but a tool to enhance their capabilities. For example, AI can handle routine queries, freeing up customer service staff to deal with more complex issues.

The use of AI in e-commerce is a journey, not a destination. As technology and customer expectations evolve, businesses must continually adapt and innovate to stay competitive.

In conclusion, AI has revolutionized e-commerce, but it requires careful implementation and ongoing management to reap its benefits and overcome its challenges. As we move into the future, the role of AI in e-commerce is set to grow, making it an essential area of understanding for anyone involved in the industry.

"Once a new technology rolls over you, if you're not part of the steamroller, you're part of the road."
- Stewart Brand

3.9 Navigating the AI Landscape in Personal Finance and Retail

The advent of AI in personal finance and retail has brought about significant changes, opening up new possibilities and challenges for both consumers and businesses. As we move towards an increasingly AI-driven future, it is crucial to understand how to navigate this landscape effectively.

Strategies for Consumers and Businesses to Navigate the AI Landscape

For consumers, the first step is to embrace the change. AI can offer personalized recommendations, automate tedious tasks, and provide insights into spending habits, making financial management easier and more efficient. However, it's essential to understand how these systems work and the data they use to make decisions.

Businesses, on the other hand, should focus on leveraging AI to improve customer experiences and operational efficiency. They should invest in AI technologies that align with their business objectives and have clear ROI. It's also important to stay updated with the latest AI trends and understand how competitors are using AI.

The Role of Education and Awareness in Maximizing the Benefits of AI

Education and awareness play a crucial role in maximizing the benefits of AI. Consumers should educate themselves about the AI tools they use, including how they work, the data they use, and the privacy implications. This knowledge will help consumers make informed decisions and use these tools effectively.

For businesses, education should focus on understanding the potential of AI and how it can be integrated into their operations. They should also educate their employees about AI and provide necessary training to ensure smooth implementation.

Preparing for Potential Risks and Challenges in the AI-Driven Future

While AI holds immense potential, it also presents certain risks and challenges. For consumers, these may include privacy concerns, data security issues, and the risk of over-reliance on AI for decision making.

Businesses, on the other hand, may face challenges related to the integration of AI into their existing systems, the cost of AI technologies, and the need for skilled personnel to manage these technologies.

To prepare for these challenges, both consumers and businesses should stay informed about the latest developments in AI and understand the potential risks. They should also have a contingency plan in place to deal with any issues that may arise.

In conclusion, navigating the AI landscape in personal finance and retail requires a proactive approach, a willingness to learn, and an understanding of the potential risks and rewards. By staying informed and prepared, consumers and businesses can make the most of the opportunities offered by AI while mitigating potential risks.

"Navigating the AI landscape requires not just technological savvy, but a vision for a better tomorrow."
- Dennis Frank

3.10 Conclusion: Embracing the AI Revolution in Personal Finance and Retail

As we conclude this module, it's crucial to recap the key points we've covered and understand the significance of staying updated with AI developments in personal finance and retail. Let's also take a moment to look ahead at the future of AI in these sectors.

Recap of Key Points

Throughout this module, we've explored the transformative role of AI in personal finance and retail. We've seen how AI is revolutionizing personal finance, making it easier for individuals to manage their finances, make informed investment decisions, and plan for the future. In retail, AI is changing the shopping experience, providing personalized recommendations, streamlining logistics, and improving customer service.

We also delved into the benefits, challenges, and risks of AI in these sectors. We discussed how AI can improve efficiency, accuracy, and customer satisfaction, but also raise concerns about data privacy, job displacement, and the digital divide.

The Importance of Staying Abreast of AI Developments

As AI continues to evolve and permeate these sectors, it's essential for both consumers and businesses to stay abreast of these developments. For consumers, understanding AI can help them take full advantage of AI-powered tools and services, make informed decisions, and protect their privacy. For businesses, staying updated with AI developments is crucial for maintaining competitiveness, improving services, and meeting customer expectations.

Looking Ahead: The Future of AI in Personal Finance and Retail

Looking ahead, the future of AI in personal finance and retail is exciting and full of potential. We can expect more sophisticated AI tools for personal finance management, offering more personalized and proactive financial advice. In retail, we may see more immersive AI-powered shopping experiences, with virtual reality (VR) and augmented reality (AR) technologies playing a significant role.

However, as AI becomes more prevalent, it's also important to address the challenges and risks it brings. It's crucial to ensure that AI is used ethically and responsibly, with proper safeguards for data privacy and security. Moreover, as AI reshapes the job landscape, it's important to provide education and training opportunities for workers to adapt to the AI-driven future.

In conclusion, embracing the AI revolution in personal finance and retail is not just about adopting new technologies, but also about understanding their implications, adapting to changes, and navigating the challenges and opportunities they present. As we move forward, let's continue to explore, learn, and adapt to the AI-driven world, and harness its potential to enhance our lives and societies.

"For a successful technology, reality must take precedence over public relations, for nature cannot be fooled."
- Richard P. Feynman

4.1 Understanding AI in Healthcare

Welcome to the first lesson of our module on "Healthcare in the Age of AI". In this lesson, we will be exploring the concept of Artificial Intelligence (AI) in the healthcare sector, its role, potential, evolution, and some of its applications.

The Concept of AI in Healthcare

Artificial Intelligence (AI) in healthcare refers to the use of complex algorithms and software to emulate human cognition in the analysis, interpretation, and comprehension of complicated medical and healthcare data. Specifically, AI is the ability for computer algorithms to approximate conclusions without direct human input.

The Role and Potential of AI in Healthcare

The primary aim of health-related AI applications is to analyze relationships between prevention or treatment techniques and patient outcomes. AI programs have been developed and applied to practices such as diagnosis processes, treatment protocol development, drug development, personalized medicine, and patient monitoring and care.

AI has the potential to significantly improve patient outcomes by enabling earlier diagnosis of complications and improved treatment of diseases. It can also help to reduce the cost of healthcare by automating routine tasks, such as data analysis, which can free up healthcare professionals to focus on patient care.

The Evolution of AI in Healthcare

AI in healthcare has evolved significantly over the years. In the early stages, AI was primarily used to automate administrative tasks. However, with the advent of more sophisticated AI technologies, such as machine learning and natural language processing, AI's role in healthcare has expanded to include more complex tasks such as diagnosing diseases, suggesting treatments, and predicting patient outcomes.

Today, AI is being used in various aspects of healthcare, from radiology to drug discovery, and its use is expected to grow as the technology advances.

Overview of AI Applications in Healthcare

AI has a wide range of applications in healthcare. Here are a few examples:

- **Predictive Analytics**: AI can be used to predict patient outcomes based on their health data and can help doctors make better treatment decisions.

- **Imaging and Diagnostics**: AI can help interpret medical images, such as X-rays and MRIs, more accurately and quickly than human radiologists.

- **Personalized Medicine**: AI can help doctors develop personalized treatment plans based on a patient's genetic makeup.

- **Drug Discovery**: AI can help in the discovery of new drugs by analyzing large amounts of biomedical data.

In conclusion, AI has the potential to revolutionize the healthcare industry by improving patient outcomes, reducing costs, and making healthcare more personalized. However, it also presents new challenges that need to be addressed, such as data privacy and the need for regulation. In the next lessons, we will delve deeper into these topics and explore how AI is transforming various aspects of healthcare.

"AI is not about replacing human thought but about enhancing the canvas on which it paints its ideas."
- Dennis Frank

4.2 AI in Diagnosis

Introduction

Artificial Intelligence (AI) has emerged as a powerful tool in healthcare, particularly in the realm of disease diagnosis. By leveraging complex algorithms and machine learning, AI can analyze vast amounts of health data to detect patterns, make predictions, and aid in the diagnostic process. Let's delve into how AI is revolutionizing disease diagnosis, the benefits it brings, real-world case studies, and the challenges it poses.

How AI is Used in Disease Diagnosis

AI's role in disease diagnosis primarily revolves around analyzing medical images, patient data, and genetic information to detect signs of diseases. Machine learning algorithms can be trained to recognize patterns in CT scans, MRIs, X-rays, and other imaging data to identify abnormalities such as tumors, fractures, or signs of diseases like pneumonia or Alzheimer's. Additionally, AI can analyze electronic health records, lab results, and other patient data to predict disease risks and support early detection.

Benefits of AI in Improving Diagnostic Accuracy

AI brings several benefits to disease diagnosis. Firstly, it can significantly improve diagnostic accuracy. Machine learning algorithms can analyze data with a level of detail and speed that is beyond human capabilities, reducing the likelihood of errors and missed diagnoses. Secondly, AI can support early detection of diseases, which is crucial for effective treatment and improved patient outcomes. Lastly, AI can help reduce the workload of healthcare professionals, allowing them to focus more on patient care.

Case Studies of AI in Diagnosis

Several real-world examples illustrate the potential of AI in disease diagnosis. Google's DeepMind developed an AI system that can diagnose eye diseases by analyzing retinal scans with an accuracy comparable to human experts. Another example is IBM's Watson for Oncology, which uses AI to analyze medical literature, patient records, and other data to provide treatment recommendations for cancer patients. These case studies highlight the transformative potential of AI in healthcare.

Challenges and Limitations of AI in Diagnosis

Despite its potential, AI in disease diagnosis also poses several challenges. One major concern is data privacy and security, as AI systems require access to sensitive patient data. Another challenge is the risk of algorithmic bias, which can lead to disparities in healthcare outcomes. Furthermore, AI systems are only as good as the data they're trained on, and any inaccuracies in the training data can lead to errors in diagnosis. Lastly, there's a need for clear regulatory guidelines to ensure the safe and ethical use of AI in healthcare.

Conclusion

AI holds immense potential in transforming disease diagnosis, offering improved accuracy, early detection, and more efficient healthcare delivery. However, it's crucial to address the challenges it poses to ensure its benefits are realized while mitigating potential risks. As we continue to navigate the AI revolution in healthcare, it's clear that AI will play a pivotal role in shaping the future of disease diagnosis.

In the next lesson, we will explore the role of AI in treatment planning, another critical aspect of healthcare that's being transformed by AI. Stay tuned to learn more about the exciting world of AI in healthcare.

"Technology is best when it brings people together." - Matt Mullenweg

4.3 AI in Treatment Planning

Artificial Intelligence (AI) is playing an increasingly important role in healthcare, particularly in the realm of treatment planning. In this lesson, we will explore how AI is being used to create personalized treatment plans, predict treatment outcomes, and the ethical considerations that arise in AI-driven treatment planning.

Role of AI in Creating Personalized Treatment Plans

AI is revolutionizing the way we approach treatment planning by enabling highly personalized treatment plans. These plans are tailored to the individual patient's unique genetic makeup, lifestyle, and other factors. AI algorithms analyze vast amounts of data, including medical history, genetic data, and lifestyle factors, to identify the most effective treatment options for each patient. This level of personalization can significantly improve treatment effectiveness and patient outcomes.

AI in Predicting Treatment Outcomes

Predicting treatment outcomes is another area where AI is making significant strides. AI algorithms can analyze data from past treatments, including patient responses and outcomes, to predict how a patient will respond to a particular treatment plan. This predictive ability can help doctors make more informed decisions about treatment options and manage potential risks more effectively. For example, if an AI algorithm predicts a high risk of adverse reactions to a particular medication, doctors can explore alternative treatments.

Case Studies of AI in Treatment Planning

There are numerous examples of how AI is being used in treatment planning across various medical fields. One such example is in the field of oncology, where AI is being used to create personalized treatment plans for cancer patients. By analyzing a patient's genetic data, AI can identify the most effective treatment options, reducing the trial-and-error approach often used in cancer treatment.

Another example is in the field of mental health, where AI is being used to predict treatment outcomes for patients with depression. By analyzing data from previous patients, including their responses to different treatments, AI can help doctors identify the most effective treatment options for each individual patient.

Ethical Considerations in AI-Driven Treatment Planning

While the use of AI in treatment planning offers many benefits, it also raises several ethical considerations. One of the primary concerns is data privacy. The use of AI in treatment planning requires the collection and analysis of vast amounts of personal data, raising concerns about how this data is stored, used, and protected.

Another ethical consideration is the potential for AI to exacerbate health disparities. If AI algorithms are trained on data that is not representative of all patient populations, they may be less effective for underrepresented groups. This could potentially lead to worse treatment outcomes for these groups.

In conclusion, AI is transforming treatment planning in healthcare, offering the potential for more personalized and effective treatment plans. However, as we continue to navigate this new landscape, it is crucial to consider the ethical implications and strive for a future where AI benefits all patients equally.

In the next lesson, we will explore the role of AI in patient monitoring and care.

"The purpose of technology is not to confuse the brain but to serve the body." - William S. Burroughs

4.4 AI in Patient Monitoring and Care

In this lesson, we will explore the role of AI in patient monitoring and care, a critical aspect of healthcare. We'll delve into how AI is revolutionizing patient care, from monitoring systems to telemedicine and home healthcare.

AI in Patient Monitoring Systems

AI has a significant role in patient monitoring systems, enhancing the accuracy and efficiency of healthcare services. These systems utilize AI algorithms to analyze patient data in real-time, enabling healthcare providers to track vital signs and detect anomalies promptly. AI-powered monitoring systems can predict potential health risks, allowing for preventative measures and timely interventions.

For example, AI can monitor heart rate variability, blood pressure, and oxygen levels, alerting healthcare providers if there's a significant deviation from the normal range. This proactive approach can save lives, particularly in critical care situations.

AI in Telemedicine and Virtual Care

The advent of AI has also transformed telemedicine and virtual care, making healthcare more accessible. AI-powered chatbots and virtual assistants can provide medical advice, schedule appointments, and even assist in diagnosing illnesses based on symptoms described by patients.

Furthermore, AI can enhance video consultations by providing real-time data analysis and recommendations, supporting healthcare professionals in delivering remote care. In a world where remote consultations are becoming increasingly necessary, AI's role in telemedicine is invaluable.

AI in Home Healthcare and Elderly Care

AI's impact extends to home healthcare and elderly care as well. AI-enabled devices can assist in medication management, monitor daily activities, and alert caregivers in case of emergencies. For instance, AI-powered wearable devices can track an elderly person's movement, detecting falls or unusual behavior patterns.

In home healthcare, AI can help patients manage chronic conditions, providing reminders for medication, and monitoring health parameters. This not only enhances the quality of care but also empowers patients, promoting independence and improving their quality of life.

Challenges and Opportunities in AI-Driven Patient Care

Despite the numerous benefits, AI-driven patient care also presents several challenges. These include concerns about data privacy, the need for regulatory oversight, and the risk of over-reliance on technology. It's crucial to address these challenges to harness the full potential of AI in patient care.

On the other hand, AI offers immense opportunities for improving patient care. It can make healthcare more personalized, predictive, and proactive. As we continue to advance in AI technology, we can expect even more innovative solutions that enhance patient monitoring and care.

In conclusion, AI is playing a pivotal role in transforming patient care, making it more efficient, accessible, and personalized. As we navigate the AI revolution in healthcare, it's essential to embrace these changes while also addressing the associated challenges. By doing so, we can ensure that AI serves as a powerful tool in enhancing healthcare outcomes and improving patient lives.

In the next lesson, we will explore another exciting aspect of AI in healthcare - its role in medical research and drug discovery.

"The great myth of our times is that technology is communication."
- Libby Larsen

4.5 AI in Medical Research and Drug Discovery

AI in Medical Research and Clinical Trials

Artificial Intelligence (AI) is playing a crucial role in modern medical research, particularly in the design and execution of clinical trials. Clinical trials are the backbone of medical research, determining the safety and efficacy of new treatments. Traditionally, these trials have been time-consuming and costly, but AI is changing the game.

AI algorithms can analyze vast amounts of data to identify suitable candidates for clinical trials, reducing the time it takes to recruit participants. Furthermore, AI can monitor the progress of trials in real-time, identifying any potential issues or side effects much quicker than traditional methods. This not only speeds up the research process but also enhances the safety of trial participants.

AI in Drug Discovery and Development

The process of drug discovery and development is another area where AI is making a significant impact. The traditional drug discovery process is a long and expensive one, often taking years and billions of dollars to bring a new drug to market.

AI is being used to streamline this process in several ways. For instance, AI algorithms can analyze vast databases of chemical compounds to identify potential new drugs, a process that would take humans years to complete. AI can also predict how these compounds will interact with the human body, helping to identify potential side effects early in the development process.

Moreover, AI can also help in the process of drug repurposing - finding new uses for existing drugs. This can significantly reduce the time and cost associated with bringing a new treatment to market.

Case Studies of AI in Medical Research

Several companies and institutions are already harnessing the power of AI in medical research. For example, Google's DeepMind has developed an AI system called AlphaFold, which can predict the 3D structure of proteins with remarkable accuracy. This has huge implications for drug discovery, as understanding protein structures is key to developing new treatments.

Another example is the use of AI by pharmaceutical giant Pfizer. The company uses AI to analyze real-world data from electronic health records and insurance claims to identify potential new uses for existing drugs.

Future of AI in Medical Research and Drug Discovery

The future of AI in medical research and drug discovery looks promising. As AI algorithms become more sophisticated, they will be able to analyze more complex data and make more accurate predictions. This could lead to the discovery of new treatments for diseases that currently have no cure.

However, as with all AI applications, there are challenges to overcome. These include issues around data privacy and the need for robust validation of AI algorithms. Despite these challenges, the potential benefits of AI in medical research and drug discovery are enormous, and it's an area that's set to continue to grow in the coming years.

In conclusion, AI is revolutionizing medical research and drug discovery, making the process faster, more efficient, and potentially more successful. By embracing this technology, we can look forward to a future where new treatments are discovered more quickly, benefiting patients worldwide.

"Our technology forces us to live mythically." - Marshall McLuhan

4.6 AI in Healthcare Administration

Artificial Intelligence (AI) is not just making waves in diagnosis and treatment within the healthcare sector. It is also revolutionizing healthcare administration, bringing about significant changes in how healthcare facilities are managed. This lesson aims to shed light on the role of AI in healthcare administration and management, how it aids in healthcare data management, its potential in improving healthcare efficiency and reducing costs, and the challenges that come with its implementation.

Role of AI in Healthcare Administration and Management

AI is proving to be a game-changer in healthcare administration. It's helping to streamline administrative tasks, such as scheduling appointments, managing patient records, and handling billing. AI-powered chatbots, for instance, can handle routine inquiries, freeing up staff to focus on more complex tasks. AI can also help manage and allocate resources more effectively, ensuring that healthcare facilities run smoothly.

AI in Healthcare Data Management

Healthcare facilities generate vast amounts of data daily. Managing this data can be a daunting task. AI comes in handy in this regard, as it can quickly analyze and interpret large datasets. AI can identify patterns and trends in the data, providing valuable insights that can improve patient care. For example, AI can help predict patient admission rates, helping hospitals manage their resources more effectively.

AI in Improving Healthcare Efficiency and Reducing Costs

AI can significantly improve efficiency in healthcare administration. By automating routine tasks, AI can reduce the workload on healthcare staff, allowing them to focus on patient care. This increased efficiency can lead to reduced operational costs, as less time and resources are wasted on administrative tasks. Moreover, AI can help reduce errors in billing and record-keeping, further saving costs.

Challenges in Implementing AI in Healthcare Administration

Despite its potential, implementing AI in healthcare administration comes with its challenges. One of the main issues is data privacy. With AI handling sensitive patient data, there are concerns about how this data is stored and used. There's also the challenge of integrating AI into existing systems. Healthcare facilities may need to overhaul their current systems, which can be costly and time-consuming. Additionally, there's a need for training staff to use AI systems, which can also pose a challenge.

In conclusion, AI has the potential to transform healthcare administration, making it more efficient and cost-effective. However, it's essential to address the challenges that come with its implementation to fully harness its benefits. As we move forward, it will be interesting to see how AI continues to shape the future of healthcare administration.

4.7 Ethical and Legal Implications of AI in Healthcare

Let's delve into the ethical and legal implications of AI in healthcare. As AI continues to revolutionize healthcare, it's crucial to understand the ethical considerations and legal regulations that come with this transformation.

Ethical Considerations in AI-Driven Healthcare

AI's potential to improve healthcare is immense, but it also raises several ethical questions.

AI Bias and Discrimination

AI systems are trained on vast amounts of data, and if this data is biased, the AI system can also become biased, leading to unequal healthcare outcomes. For instance, if an AI system is trained mostly on data from a particular demographic, its performance may be less accurate for other demographics.

Informed Consent

AI can process and analyze patient data in ways that were unimaginable a few years ago. But how should informed consent be obtained when AI is involved? And how can patients understand and consent to complex AI processes?

Privacy and Data Security

As AI systems need large amounts of data to function effectively, there are concerns about patient privacy and data security. How can we ensure that patient data is used responsibly and securely?

Legal Implications and Regulations of AI in Healthcare

AI in healthcare also presents several legal challenges.

Liability

If an AI system makes a mistake, who is liable? The healthcare provider, the AI developer, or the AI system itself?

Regulation

How should AI systems be regulated to ensure they are safe and effective? And how can regulations keep up with rapidly advancing AI technologies?

Balancing AI Innovation and Patient Rights

Striking a balance between encouraging AI innovation and protecting patient rights is a delicate task. On one hand, we want to promote the development of AI technologies that can improve healthcare. On the other hand, we must ensure that these technologies are used in a way that respects patient rights and promotes equity.

Case Studies of Ethical and Legal Dilemmas in AI Healthcare

To illustrate these ethical and legal issues, let's look at a few case studies.

Case Study 1: AI Bias

A study found that an AI system used to predict which patients would be referred to programs that aim to improve care for patients with complex medical needs was less likely to refer black people than white people. This was because the AI system was trained on cost data, and black people incurred lower costs than white people, leading to the AI system's bias.

Case Study 2: Informed Consent

A hospital used an AI system to predict which patients were likely to die soon and informed the patients' doctors of its predictions. But the hospital did not inform the patients that an AI system was used to make these predictions. This raises questions about informed consent and transparency in AI-driven healthcare.

In conclusion, as we embrace the AI revolution in healthcare, we must navigate the ethical and legal implications carefully. By doing so, we can ensure that AI is used to improve healthcare in a way that is fair, ethical, and respects patient rights.

4.8 The Future of AI in Healthcare

Emerging Trends in AI Healthcare

Artificial Intelligence (AI) is making significant strides in the healthcare industry, and the future promises even more revolutionary changes. Several emerging trends are shaping the future of AI in healthcare.

For instance, AI is increasingly being used in predictive analytics to forecast disease outbreaks and patient health risks. Machine learning algorithms are being trained on vast datasets to predict the likelihood of patients developing certain conditions, allowing for early intervention and prevention.

Another trend is the rise of AI-powered telemedicine. With the advent of AI chatbots and virtual health assistants, patients can now receive medical advice and care remotely, making healthcare more accessible, especially in underserved areas.

In the realm of medical imaging, AI is being used to detect anomalies in scans with a level of accuracy that rivals, and in some cases surpasses, human experts. This can significantly speed up the diagnosis process and improve patient outcomes.

Potential Impact of AI on Healthcare Outcomes

AI has the potential to significantly improve healthcare outcomes. By enabling early detection and diagnosis, AI can help reduce the severity of diseases and improve survival rates. AI can also personalize treatment plans based on a patient's unique genetic makeup and health history, improving the effectiveness of treatments.

AI can also streamline healthcare administration, reducing the burden on healthcare professionals and allowing them to focus more on patient care. By automating routine tasks, AI can help reduce errors and improve efficiency in healthcare delivery.

Moreover, AI can democratize healthcare by making it more accessible. AI-powered telemedicine can bring healthcare services to remote areas and underserved populations, reducing health disparities.

Preparing for the Future of AI in Healthcare

As AI continues to transform healthcare, it's crucial for healthcare professionals and organizations to adapt and prepare for this future. This includes investing in AI education and training to understand and effectively use AI technologies. Healthcare organizations should also invest in AI infrastructure, including data management systems and AI hardware and software.

Moreover, healthcare professionals and organizations need to be aware of the ethical and legal implications of AI in healthcare. This includes issues related to patient privacy, data security, and the ethical use of AI.

Conclusion: Embracing AI in Healthcare

In conclusion, the future of AI in healthcare is promising, with the potential to improve healthcare outcomes, efficiency, and accessibility. However, embracing this future requires preparation, including investing in AI education and infrastructure, and addressing ethical and legal issues. As we move forward, it's crucial to navigate this AI revolution in healthcare with care and foresight, ensuring that AI is used to enhance, not replace, the human touch in healthcare.

"The dialogue between human and machine intelligence will write the story of our future." - Dennis Frank

5.1 Introduction to AI in Smart Living

In this lesson, we will introduce the concept of Smart Living, the role of Artificial Intelligence (AI) in it, and how it impacts our daily lives and routines.

Understanding the Concept of Smart Living

Smart Living refers to the use of connected, automated systems to control, monitor, and optimize functions in a home or city. These systems can manage a wide range of tasks, from controlling home appliances and security systems to managing traffic flow and energy usage in a city. The goal of Smart Living is to make our lives more convenient, our homes more comfortable and energy-efficient, and our cities more livable and sustainable.

The Role of AI in Smart Living

AI plays a crucial role in Smart Living by providing the intelligence that makes these systems "smart." AI algorithms can analyze data from various sensors and devices, learn from it, and make decisions or predictions based on it. For example, a smart thermostat can learn your daily routine and adjust the temperature in your home accordingly. Or a smart traffic management system can analyze real-time traffic data and adjust traffic light timings to optimize traffic flow.

AI can also enable more advanced features in Smart Living systems. For example, AI-powered voice assistants like Amazon's Alexa or Google Assistant can understand and respond to voice commands, allowing you to control your smart home devices with just your voice. Similarly, AI can power predictive maintenance systems in smart cities, predicting when infrastructure like roads or bridges might need repair and scheduling maintenance before a problem occurs.

The Impact of AI on Our Daily Lives and Routines

The impact of AI-powered Smart Living on our daily lives and routines can be profound. On a personal level, AI can automate routine tasks, making our lives more convenient. For example, a smart home system can automate tasks like turning lights on and off, adjusting the thermostat, or even brewing your morning coffee. This can save us time, reduce energy usage, and make our homes more comfortable.

On a larger scale, AI-powered Smart Living can make our cities more efficient and sustainable. For example, smart traffic management systems can reduce traffic congestion, making our commutes faster and less stressful. Smart energy grids can optimize energy usage, reducing waste and lowering our energy bills. And smart waste management systems can make waste collection more efficient, reducing pollution and improving public health.

In conclusion, AI is a key enabling technology for Smart Living, making our homes and cities smarter, more efficient, and more sustainable. As we move forward in this module, we will delve deeper into the various applications of AI in Smart Living, from smart homes to smart cities.

5.2 AI in Smart Homes

Introduction

Artificial Intelligence (AI) has been the driving force behind the evolution of smart homes. The concept of smart homes is no longer a futuristic idea but a reality that we live in today. This lesson explores the concept of smart homes, how AI contributes to smart homes, the benefits and challenges of AI in smart homes, and a case study of AI in home automation systems.

The Concept of Smart Homes

A smart home is a residence that uses internet-connected devices to enable the remote monitoring and management of appliances and systems, such as lighting and heating. Smart homes aim to provide their owners with increased comfort, security, energy efficiency, and convenience.

How AI Contributes to Smart Homes

AI contributes to smart homes by enabling devices to learn from homeowners' habits and adjust their functionalities accordingly. For example, a smart thermostat can learn your preferred temperature at different times of the day and adjust the heating or cooling system automatically. AI-powered virtual assistants like Amazon's Alexa or Google Assistant can control smart home devices based on voice commands, making it easier for homeowners to manage their homes.

The Benefits of AI in Smart Homes

AI in smart homes offers numerous benefits:

1. **Convenience**: AI-powered devices can automate regular home tasks, allowing homeowners to focus on other activities.

2. **Energy Efficiency**: AI can optimize the use of resources like electricity and water, leading to significant savings.

3. **Security**: AI-powered security systems can provide real-time alerts and recognize unusual activities, enhancing home security.

4. **Accessibility**: AI can assist individuals with disabilities, making smart homes more accessible.

The Challenges of AI in Smart Homes

Despite the benefits, there are also challenges associated with AI in smart homes:

1. **Privacy Concerns**: As smart devices collect data about homeowners' habits, there are concerns about data privacy and security.

2. **Dependence on Internet Connectivity**: The functionality of AI-powered devices largely depends on internet connectivity. Any disruption can impact the operation of these devices.

3. **Complexity**: Some users may find it challenging to set up and operate smart home systems.

Case Study: AI in Home Automation Systems

A prime example of AI in smart homes is the use of AI in home automation systems. These systems can control lighting, climate, entertainment systems, and appliances. They can also include home security elements such as alarm systems and access control.

For instance, Google Nest, a leading home automation system, uses AI to learn from users' behaviors and preferences. It adjusts the home's temperature based on the learned patterns, detects unusual activities in the home, and even recognizes different family members' faces with its built-in camera.

Conclusion

AI has transformed the concept of smart homes, making them more efficient, secure, and convenient. While there are challenges, the benefits of AI in smart homes far outweigh the drawbacks. As AI continues to evolve, we can expect our homes to become even smarter, further simplifying our lives.

In the next lesson, we'll explore how AI is shaping smart cities, another exciting aspect of our AI-driven future.

"Technology is teaching us to be human again." - Simon Mainwaring

5.3 AI in Smart Cities

Understanding the Concept of Smart Cities

Smart cities are urban areas that use different types of electronic methods and sensors to collect data. Insights gained from this data are used to manage assets, resources, and services efficiently. In other words, a smart city is a framework, predominantly composed of Information and Communication Technologies (ICT), to develop, deploy, and promote sustainable development practices to address growing urbanization challenges.

A big part of this ICT framework is essentially an intelligent network of connected objects and machines that transmit data using wireless technology and the cloud. In a smart city, this infrastructure oversees the proper functioning of urban services such as electricity, water supply, and transportation to ensure a better quality of life for its residents.

The Role of AI in Developing Smart Cities

Artificial Intelligence (AI) plays a crucial role in the development of smart cities. AI can analyze the vast amounts of data generated by smart cities to improve services, reduce costs, and optimize resources. Here are a few ways AI contributes to smart cities:

1. **Traffic Management**: AI can analyze traffic data in real-time to manage congestion and reduce travel times. It can also predict traffic patterns to help plan infrastructure development.

2. **Waste Management**: AI can optimize waste collection routes, reducing fuel consumption and improving efficiency.

3. **Energy Management**: AI can analyze energy usage patterns to optimize energy consumption and reduce waste.

4. **Public Safety**: AI can analyze video footage from surveillance cameras to detect anomalies and improve public safety.

5. **Urban Planning**: AI can analyze demographic and urban data to assist in urban planning and development.

The Benefits and Challenges of AI in Smart Cities

AI in smart cities brings numerous benefits, including improved efficiency, reduced environmental impact, and enhanced quality of life for residents. However, it also presents challenges, such as data privacy concerns, the need for significant infrastructure investment, and the risk of job displacement due to automation.

Case Study: AI in Urban Planning and Management

Let's look at a case study that illustrates the role of AI in urban planning and management. The city of Barcelona, Spain, has been a pioneer in using AI to improve urban life. The city has implemented a system called "Sentilo," which collects data from thousands of sensors located around the city. The data is then analyzed using AI to improve services such as waste management, parking, and environmental monitoring. This has led to significant improvements in efficiency and quality of life in Barcelona.

In conclusion, AI plays a crucial role in the development of smart cities, offering numerous benefits but also presenting challenges that need to be addressed. As AI continues to evolve, it will undoubtedly play an increasingly important role in shaping the cities of the future.

"In the symphony of AI, each algorithm is a note, playing its part in harmonizing the future."
- Dennis Frank

5.4 AI in Energy Management

In this lesson, we will delve into how Artificial Intelligence (AI) is revolutionizing energy management in our homes and cities. We will explore the role of AI in energy conservation and efficiency and look at a case study on AI in Smart Grids.

The Role of AI in Energy Management in Homes and Cities

Artificial Intelligence is playing a significant role in energy management, both in our homes and in our cities. AI systems are being used to optimize energy consumption, reduce waste, and increase efficiency.

In our homes, AI-powered devices like smart thermostats and smart appliances can learn our habits and preferences, adjusting energy usage accordingly to save power. For instance, a smart thermostat can learn your schedule and adjust the temperature when you're not home, saving energy without sacrificing comfort.

In our cities, AI is being used in a variety of ways to manage energy. For example, AI can optimize street lighting based on traffic and pedestrian patterns, reducing energy waste. AI can also predict energy demand based on weather patterns, time of day, and other factors, helping to balance the power grid and prevent blackouts.

How AI Can Help in Energy Conservation and Efficiency

AI can help in energy conservation and efficiency in several ways. By learning patterns and making predictions, AI can optimize energy usage and reduce waste. This can result in significant energy savings and a reduction in carbon emissions.

AI can also help identify energy inefficiencies. For example, AI can analyze energy usage data to identify patterns that indicate energy waste, such as appliances that are using more power than they should. This can help homeowners and city officials take steps to improve energy efficiency.

Furthermore, AI can help integrate renewable energy sources into the power grid. AI can predict the output of wind and solar power based on weather forecasts, helping to balance the power grid and reduce reliance on fossil fuels.

Case Study: AI in Smart Grids

Smart Grids are a perfect example of how AI is being used in energy management. A Smart Grid uses AI and other advanced technologies to monitor and manage the flow of electricity from all generation sources to meet the varying electricity demands of end users.

AI can analyze data from the grid to predict energy demand, optimize energy distribution, and prevent blackouts. It can also help integrate renewable energy sources into the grid, balancing supply and demand to reduce reliance on fossil fuels.

For instance, Google's DeepMind has used machine learning to predict the wind power output 36 hours in advance, allowing the energy grid to better plan how to use this power. This has increased the value of wind energy by roughly 20%.

In conclusion, AI is playing a crucial role in energy manage-ment, helping us to conserve energy and increase efficiency in our homes and cities. As we continue to face the challenges of climate change, AI will be an essential tool in our efforts to create a more sustainable future.

In the next lesson, we will explore how AI is used in security and surveillance.

"We are stuck with technology when what we really want is just stuff that works." - Douglas Adams

5.5 AI in Security and Surveillance

Introduction

As we delve further into the realm of smart living, it becomes essential to discuss the role of Artificial Intelligence (AI) in security and surveillance. AI has been a game-changer in this field, providing enhanced security measures in homes and cities while offering a new level of convenience and peace of mind.

The Role of AI in Enhancing Security in Homes and Cities

AI has revolutionized the way we approach security in our homes and cities. With the advent of AI, security systems have become smarter and more efficient. They can now analyze patterns, recognize faces, and even detect suspicious activities.

AI-powered security systems in homes can alert homeowners of any unusual activity, even when they are not at home. They can distinguish between residents and strangers, reducing false alarms and ensuring that only genuine threats are reported.

In cities, AI can help monitor public spaces, detect anomalies, and respond to threats more quickly and effectively. From traffic management to crowd control during public events, AI plays a crucial role in maintaining the safety and security of urban spaces.

The Impact of AI on Surveillance Systems

AI has brought about significant changes in surveillance systems. Traditional surveillance systems relied on human monitoring, which was prone to errors and inefficiencies. AI, on the other hand, can process and analyze vast amounts of data in real-time, making surveillance more accurate and reliable.

AI in surveillance systems can help in object recognition, anomaly detection, and behavior analysis. It can identify individuals, vehicles, and even detect suspicious activities or behaviors. This not only enhances security but also helps in proactive threat management.

Case Study: AI in Home Security Systems

Let's consider a practical example of how AI is transforming home security systems. Modern AI-based home security systems, such as those offered by companies like Ring and Nest, use advanced AI algorithms for facial recognition and anomaly detection.

These systems can distinguish between known and unknown faces, reducing false alarms from friends and family members. They can also detect unusual activities, such as an unknown person loitering near your home, and send real-time alerts to your smartphone.

Furthermore, these systems can learn from their environment and adapt over time. For instance, they can learn to ignore a pet's movement while focusing on human activity, making them smarter and more efficient with each passing day.

Conclusion

AI's role in security and surveillance is a testament to its potential in transforming our lives. As we continue to embrace smart living, AI will undoubtedly play an increasingly significant role in ensuring our safety and security. As we adapt to this AI-driven era, it's crucial to understand and leverage these advancements for a safer and more secure future.

In the next lesson, we will explore how AI is revolutionizing energy management in homes and cities.

"The true art of AI is not in coding, but in understanding the heartbeat of humanity." - Dennis Frank

5.6 AI in Transportation and Traffic Management

Introduction

Artificial Intelligence (AI) has started to play a significant role in the transportation sector, transforming the way we commute and manage traffic. From autonomous vehicles to smart traffic control systems, AI is revolutionizing our transportation systems, making them more efficient, safe, and sustainable. In this lesson, we'll delve into how AI is improving transportation in cities and managing traffic to reduce congestion.

The Role of AI in Improving Transportation in Cities

AI is being increasingly used to make transportation more efficient and convenient. It is at the heart of autonomous vehicles, which can sense their environment and moving safely with little or no human input. These vehicles use AI algorithms to process data from sensors and make decisions about steering, acceleration, and braking.

AI is also being used to optimize public transportation systems. For example, AI algorithms can analyze data from various sources, such as GPS trackers on buses and trains, to predict arrival times more accurately, improving the reliability of public transportation.

122

Moreover, AI can help in planning and managing transportation infrastructure. By analyzing traffic data, AI can identify patterns and trends, helping city planners make informed decisions about where to build new roads or public transportation routes.

AI in Managing Traffic and Reducing Congestion

Traffic congestion is a major issue in many cities, leading to wasted time, increased pollution, and stress for drivers. AI can help address this problem in several ways.

Firstly, AI can be used to optimize traffic signal timings. Traditional traffic lights operate on fixed schedules, which can lead to unnecessary delays. AI can analyze real-time traffic data to adjust signal timings dynamically, reducing delays and improving traffic flow.

Secondly, AI can predict traffic congestion before it happens. By analyzing data from various sources, such as weather forecasts, social media posts, and historical traffic data, AI can forecast traffic conditions and suggest alternative routes to drivers.

Finally, AI can help manage traffic incidents more effectively. For example, AI can analyze data from traffic cameras to detect accidents or roadworks and alert drivers in real-time, helping to reduce congestion.

Case Study: AI in Autonomous Vehicles and Traffic Control Systems

Let's look at a couple of examples of how AI is being used in transportation and traffic management.

Autonomous Vehicles: Companies like Tesla and Waymo are using AI to develop self-driving cars. These vehicles use a combination of sensors, such as cameras, radar, and Lidar, to perceive their environment. AI algorithms process this data and make decisions about how to navigate the vehicle safely and efficiently.

Traffic Control Systems: Cities like Pittsburgh in the USA are using AI to optimize traffic signal timings. The system, developed by a company called Surtrac, uses AI to analyze real-time traffic data and adjust signal timings dynamically. This has resulted in a significant reduction in travel times and vehicle emissions.

Conclusion

AI holds great promise for improving transportation and managing traffic in our cities. By making our transportation systems more efficient and reducing congestion, AI can help make our cities more livable and sustainable. However, the widespread adoption of AI in transportation also raises several challenges, such as ensuring the safety of autonomous vehicles and protecting the privacy of individuals. As we move forward, it will be essential to navigate these challenges carefully to realize the full potential of AI in transportation and traffic management.

5.7 AI in Waste Management

The Role of AI in Managing Waste in Homes and Cities

Artificial Intelligence (AI) is revolutionizing the way we manage waste in our homes and cities. Through the use of smart sensors, AI algorithms, and data analytics, waste management has become more efficient and effective.

For instance, AI can be used to sort waste more accurately, reducing the amount of waste that ends up in landfills. In cities, AI can optimize waste collection routes, reducing fuel consumption and improving the efficiency of waste collection services.

How AI Contributes to Sustainable Waste Management Practices

AI holds the potential to significantly contribute to sustainable waste management practices. By accurately sorting waste, AI can increase the amount of waste that can be recycled or composted, reducing the environmental impact of waste.

Moreover, AI can predict waste generation patterns, allowing for more effective planning and implementation of waste management strategies. This not only reduces the cost of waste management but also minimizes the environmental footprint of waste disposal.

AI also plays a crucial role in reducing e-waste by identifying and extracting valuable materials from electronic waste, which can then be reused or recycled.

Case Study: AI in Smart Waste Management Systems

Let's delve into a practical example of AI in waste management. One innovative company, Greyparrot, has developed an AI-powered waste recognition system. This system uses computer vision to identify different types of waste on a conveyor belt in real-time, improving the accuracy and efficiency of waste sorting.

Another example is the use of AI in smart bins. These bins are equipped with sensors that can detect when they are full and send a signal to the waste collection agency. This ensures timely collection of waste and prevents overflow, contributing to cleaner cities.

Furthermore, companies like Waste Robotics use AI and robotics to automate the sorting of waste. Their robots can identify and sort various types of waste, including metals, plastics, and paper, making recycling processes more efficient.

Conclusion

In conclusion, AI is playing a transformative role in waste management, making it more efficient, sustainable, and cost-effective. As we continue to innovate and develop new AI technologies, we can expect to see even more improvements in the way we manage waste. This will not only benefit our homes and cities but also contribute to a more sustainable and environmentally friendly future.

In the next lesson, we will explore how AI is used in emergency response and disaster management, another crucial aspect of smart living.

"We are approaching a time when machines will be able to outperform humans at almost any task... Society needs to confront this question before it is upon us: If machines are capable of doing almost any work humans can do, what will humans do?"
- Moshe Vardi

5.8 AI in Emergency Response and Disaster Management

Introduction

Artificial Intelligence (AI) is playing an increasingly crucial role in improving emergency response and disaster management in cities around the world. By leveraging AI's predictive capabilities and real-time data analysis, cities can better prepare for disasters, respond to emergencies more efficiently, and ultimately save more lives.

The Role of AI in Emergency Response

AI can significantly enhance emergency response operations. Here's how:

- **Predictive Analysis**: AI can analyze vast amounts of data from various sources, such as weather reports, social media, and sensor data, to predict potential emergencies. This allows emergency services to prepare in advance, thereby reducing response times.

- **Real-time Data Analysis**: During an emergency, AI can analyze real-time data to provide emergency services with up-to-date information, helping them make informed decisions quickly.

- **Automation of Emergency Calls**: AI can automate the process of receiving and categorizing emergency calls, ensuring that help is dispatched efficiently and effectively.

- **Resource Allocation**: AI can help determine the optimal allocation of resources during an emergency, ensuring that help reaches where it's needed most.

Case Study: AI in Predictive Analysis for Disaster Management

Let's look at a practical example of how AI is used in disaster management.

In 2018, Google's AI division, DeepMind, partnered with the U.S. National Oceanic and Atmospheric Administration (NOAA) to improve the accuracy of weather forecasts. Using a machine learning model, they were able to predict rainfall up to six hours in advance with a significantly higher degree of accuracy than traditional methods. This allowed for better preparation and response to potential flooding, a common and often devastating disaster.

Conclusion

AI's role in emergency response and disaster management is a testament to its potential in creating smarter, safer cities. By leveraging AI, we can better predict, prepare for, and respond to emergencies, ultimately protecting lives and property. As AI technology continues to advance, its role in emergency response and disaster management is set to become even more significant.

In the next lesson, we will explore how AI is used in waste management, another crucial aspect of creating smart, efficient cities.

5.9 The Future of AI in Smart Living

In this session, we'll be looking ahead, exploring the future trends of AI in smart living and discussing their potential impacts on our lives and cities.

Predicting the Future Trends in AI for Smart Living

AI technology is rapidly evolving, and its applications in smart living are expected to expand significantly in the coming years. Here are some of the key trends we can anticipate:

1. **Increased Automation**: As AI becomes more sophisticated, we can expect to see a rise in automation within our homes and cities. From self-cleaning homes to automated traffic management systems, AI will take over many tasks, freeing up our time and making our lives more convenient.

2. **Personalized AI**: AI systems will become more personalized, learning from our habits and preferences to provide tailored services. For instance, your smart home might learn your daily routine and automatically adjust the lighting, temperature, and even music to your liking.

3. **AI and IoT Integration**: The integration of AI with the Internet of Things (IoT) will lead to more

interconnected and intelligent devices. This could range from smart refrigerators that can order groceries when you're running low, to city-wide systems that can monitor and respond to environmental changes in real-time.

4. **Energy Efficiency**: AI will play a crucial role in managing energy consumption, optimizing the use of resources, and promoting sustainability in our homes and cities.

5. **Enhanced Security**: AI will enhance security systems, using facial recognition, anomaly detection, and predictive analytics to protect our homes and cities.

The Potential Impact of These Trends on Our Lives and Cities

These trends in AI for smart living will have profound impacts on our lives and cities:

1. **Improved Quality of Life**: Increased automation and personalization will make our daily routines more convenient and enjoyable, improving our overall quality of life.

2. **Efficient Cities**: AI will make our cities more efficient, reducing traffic congestion, improving waste management, and enhancing public services.

3. **Sustainable Living**: By optimizing energy consumption, AI will contribute to more sustainable homes and cities, helping us combat climate change.

4. **Increased Safety**: Enhanced security systems will make our homes and cities safer, providing peace of mind for residents.

Preparing for the Future of AI in Smart Living

As we look forward to these exciting developments, it's important to prepare for the future of AI in smart living. This includes staying informed about new technologies, understanding their implications, and considering how we can adapt to and benefit from these changes.

In the next lesson, we'll explore how to navigate the AI landscape in smart living, providing practical tips and resources to help you embrace the AI revolution in your home and city.

In conclusion, the future of AI in smart living holds immense promise. As AI continues to evolve and integrate into our homes and cities, we can look forward to a future of increased convenience, efficiency, sustainability, and security. By staying informed and adaptable, we can make the most of these exciting developments and thrive in the AI era.

In the next and final lesson of this module, we will discuss how to navigate the AI landscape in smart living.

5.10 Navigating the AI Landscape in Smart Living

Understanding the Ethical and Privacy Implications of AI in Smart Living

Artificial Intelligence (AI) is increasingly becoming an integral part of our homes and cities, making our lives more convenient and efficient. However, this advancement comes with its own set of ethical and privacy implications.

AI in smart living often involves the collection and analysis of personal data to function effectively. For instance, smart home devices like Amazon's Alexa or Google Home collect data about your habits and preferences to provide personalized services. Similarly, AI in smart cities might involve surveillance systems that monitor public spaces to improve security or manage traffic.

While these applications of AI can greatly enhance our quality of life, they also raise important questions about privacy and consent. Who has access to the data these systems collect? How is this data being used and stored? Are individuals aware of the extent of data collection and do they have a choice in it? These are some of the ethical and privacy implications we need to consider as we navigate the AI landscape in smart living.

Strategies for Navigating These Challenges

Navigating the ethical and privacy challenges of AI in smart living requires a proactive and informed approach. Here are some strategies that can help:

1. **Stay Informed**: Understand the capabilities and limitations of the AI technologies you use. Read the privacy policies and terms of use of smart devices and services to know what data they collect and how they use it.

2. **Exercise Control**: Use the privacy settings of smart devices and services to control what data you share. You can often customize these settings to balance convenience and privacy according to your comfort level.

3. **Advocate for Transparency**: Support initiatives that promote transparency in AI. This can involve advocating for laws and regulations that require companies to disclose how they use AI and the data they collect.

4. **Promote Ethical AI Practices**: Encourage the development and use of AI that respects user privacy and consent. This can involve supporting companies that prioritize ethical AI practices and boycotting those that don't.

Conclusion: Embracing the AI Revolution in Smart Living

AI has the potential to revolutionize our homes and cities, making them more convenient, efficient, and responsive to our needs. However, as we embrace this revolution, it's crucial to navigate the ethical and privacy challenges it presents. By staying informed, exercising control, advocating for transparency, and promoting ethical AI practices, we can ensure that the AI revolution in smart living is not just smart, but also respectful of our rights and values.

"AI does not have to be evil to destroy humanity – if AI has a goal and humanity just happens in the way, it will destroy humanity as a matter of course without even thinking about it. No hard feelings." - Elon Musk

6.1 Understanding the AI Privacy Paradox

Introduction to the AI Privacy Paradox

The AI Privacy Paradox is a concept that has emerged as a result of the increasing use of Artificial Intelligence (AI) in our daily lives. This paradox arises from the conflict between the benefits of AI and the potential threats it poses to our privacy. On one hand, AI systems provide us with personalized experiences, convenience, and efficiency. On the other hand, these systems often require access to vast amounts of personal data, leading to concerns about privacy and data protection.

The Intersection of AI and Privacy

AI and privacy intersect in many ways. AI systems, by their very nature, rely on data to function. The more data they have, the better they can learn, adapt, and provide personalized services. However, this data often includes sensitive personal information. This intersection between AI and privacy is where the paradox lies. We want the benefits of AI, but we also want to protect our privacy.

The Role of AI in Data Collection and Analysis

AI plays a significant role in data collection and analysis. Machine learning algorithms, a subset of AI, are designed to learn from data, identify patterns, and make decisions or predictions. These algorithms can process vast amounts of data quickly and accurately, making them invaluable in many sectors, from healthcare to finance to retail.

However, the data that AI systems collect isn't always anonymous. Often, it's personal and sensitive, such as medical records, financial information, or browsing history. This data collection is necessary for AI systems to function effectively, but it also raises serious privacy concerns.

The Impact of AI on Personal Privacy

The impact of AI on personal privacy is significant. AI systems can potentially access, analyze, and store a vast amount of personal data. This data can be used to make predictions about our behavior, preferences, and even our personal life. The potential for misuse of this data is a serious concern.

Moreover, AI systems are often "black boxes," meaning their decision-making processes are not transparent. This lack of transparency can make it difficult for individuals to understand how their data is being used, further exacerbating privacy concerns.

In conclusion, while AI offers many benefits, it also poses significant privacy challenges. As we continue to integrate AI into our lives, it's crucial to understand and navigate this AI Privacy Paradox. In the following lessons, we will delve deeper into the ethical implications of AI and privacy, the legal landscape, and how we can protect personal information in the age of AI.

6.2 The Ethical Implications of AI and Privacy

The Ethical Dilemma of AI and Privacy

Artificial Intelligence (AI) is a double-edged sword. On one hand, it has the potential to revolutionize our lives, making them more convenient and efficient. On the other hand, it raises serious ethical concerns, particularly when it comes to privacy.

AI systems often rely on vast amounts of data to function effectively. This data is usually personal, collected from various sources such as social media, online searches, and even our daily interactions with AI-powered devices. While this data helps AI systems to learn and improve, it also raises questions about privacy. How much of our personal information should AI systems have access to? Who has the right to collect, store, and use this data? These are some of the ethical dilemmas that arise in the context of AI and privacy.

Balancing AI Innovation and Privacy Rights

The challenge lies in striking a balance between fostering AI innovation and protecting privacy rights. AI has immense potential to improve our lives. However, this should not come at the cost of our privacy.

We need to establish clear ethical guidelines that govern how AI systems collect, store, and use personal data. These guidelines should ensure that AI systems respect the principles of consent, transparency, and accountability. They should also provide individuals with control over their personal data, including the right to access, correct, and delete their data.

Case Study: Ethical Challenges in AI Data Collection

Let's consider a case study to understand the ethical challenges in AI data collection better.

In 2018, a scandal involving Facebook and Cambridge Analytica highlighted the ethical implications of AI and privacy. Cambridge Analytica, a political consulting firm, collected the personal data of millions of Facebook users without their consent. The firm used this data to build AI models that could predict and influence voter behavior.

This scandal raised several ethical questions. Was it ethical for Cambridge Analytica to collect and use personal data without consent? Was it ethical for Facebook to allow third parties to access user data? The scandal underscored the need for ethical guidelines that govern AI data collection and use.

Navigating Ethical Considerations in AI and Privacy

Navigating the ethical considerations in AI and privacy is not easy. It requires a multi-faceted approach that involves various stakeholders, including AI developers, users, regulators, and society at large.

AI developers should adhere to ethical guidelines that prioritize privacy. They should design AI systems that respect user privacy and provide users with control over their data.

Users, on the other hand, need to be aware of the privacy implications of using AI systems. They should make informed decisions about sharing their personal data and understand their rights in relation to data privacy.

Regulators have a crucial role to play in establishing and enforcing privacy laws that govern AI. These laws should protect individual privacy while also fostering AI innovation.

Finally, society needs to have an ongoing conversation about the ethical implications of AI and privacy. This conversation should involve a diverse range of voices and perspectives, ensuring that the development and use of AI align with our collective values and norms.

In conclusion, the ethical implications of AI and privacy are complex and multifaceted. Navigating these implications requires a balanced approach that respects individual privacy while also harnessing the potential of AI. As we move forward into the AI era, we must strive to create an ethical framework that guides the development and use of AI in a way that benefits all of society.

6.3 The Legal Landscape of AI and Privacy

Introduction to Legal Aspects of AI and Privacy

Artificial Intelligence (AI) has significantly transformed the way we live, work, and interact. However, with these advancements come complex challenges, particularly in terms of privacy and legal considerations. As AI systems become more sophisticated, they collect, analyze, and store vast amounts of personal data. This raises critical questions about privacy rights and data protection, leading us to explore the legal landscape of AI and privacy.

Data Protection Laws and AI

In response to the growing use of AI, several countries have enacted data protection laws to safeguard individuals' privacy. The General Data Protection Regulation (GDPR) in the European Union, the California Consumer Privacy Act (CCPA) in the United States, and the Personal Data Protection Act (PDPA) in Singapore are prime examples of such legislation. These laws govern how organizations collect, use, and store personal data, with stringent penalties for non-compliance.

However, these laws were not specifically designed with AI in mind, and their application to AI systems can be complex and unclear. For instance, the GDPR emphasizes transparency and the right to explanation, which can be challenging to implement given the 'black box' nature of some AI systems.

AI, Privacy, and Consent

One of the key legal considerations in AI and privacy is the issue of consent. Data protection laws generally require organizations to obtain individuals' consent before collecting and using their personal data. However, in the context of AI, what constitutes 'informed consent' can be a gray area.

AI systems often use data in ways that may not have been foreseeable at the time consent was given. Moreover, AI's complexity and the technical jargon often used in privacy policies can make it difficult for individuals to understand what they're consenting to. This raises critical questions about the adequacy of current consent mechanisms in the age of AI.

Case Study: Legal Challenges in AI Data Usage

Let's consider a case study to understand the legal challenges in AI data usage. In 2018, the GDPR fined a tech company for using personal data to train its AI system without explicit consent. The company argued that it had anonymized the data, making it GDPR compliant. However, the GDPR ruled that the company had failed to sufficiently anonymize the data, as it could still be traced back to individuals using sophisticated techniques.

This case underscores the legal complexities in AI and privacy. It highlights the need for robust data anonymization techniques in AI and the importance of clear and explicit consent mechanisms. It also underscores the need for legal frameworks that can keep pace with the rapid advancements in AI.

In conclusion, navigating the legal landscape of AI and privacy is a complex but necessary task. As AI continues to evolve, so too must our legal frameworks to ensure the protection of privacy rights in the AI era.

"Embracing AI means engaging with the future, not as passive observers, but as active creators." - Dennis Frank

6.4 AI and Data Security: Protecting Personal Information

AI and Data Security: An Overview

In the age of digital revolution, data has become the new oil. It's a valuable resource that powers our AI-driven world. However, with the increasing reliance on data, protecting it has become a significant challenge. AI, while being a part of the problem, also holds the potential to be a significant part of the solution.

Artificial Intelligence systems, by their very nature, require vast amounts of data to function effectively. This data often includes sensitive personal information, making data security a paramount concern. However, the same AI systems that need this data can also be used to protect it.

The Role of AI in Data Breaches

Unfortunately, AI's relationship with data security isn't entirely positive. As AI systems become more sophisticated, so do the methods of cybercriminals. AI can be used to automate cyber-attacks, making them more efficient and harder to detect. These AI-powered attacks can lead to significant data breaches, compromising the personal information of millions of individuals.

For instance, AI can be used to create more convincing phishing emails, automate the process of finding security vulnerabilities, or even carry out complex attacks that adapt in real-time to the defenses they encounter.

AI Solutions for Data Security

Despite the potential misuse of AI in cyber-attacks, AI also offers promising solutions for data security. AI can analyze patterns of behavior to detect anomalies that may indicate a security breach. For example, if a user who typically logs in during regular business hours suddenly starts accessing the system at odd hours, AI can flag this as suspicious activity.

AI can also be used to automate the process of patching security vulnerabilities. By continuously scanning for vulnerabilities and applying patches, AI can help prevent attacks before they happen.

Moreover, AI can be used in biometric authentication methods, such as facial recognition or fingerprint scanning, to provide a higher level of security than traditional passwords.

The Future of AI and Data Security

Looking ahead, AI is set to play an even larger role in data security. As AI systems become more sophisticated, they will be able to detect and respond to threats more quickly and accurately. We can also expect to see more advanced biometric authentication methods and more robust defenses against AI-powered cyber-attacks.

However, the increasing use of AI in data security also raises new challenges. For instance, as AI systems become more integral to data security, they also become more attractive targets for cybercriminals. Therefore, securing these AI systems themselves will become a crucial task.

In conclusion, while AI presents new challenges in data security, it also offers innovative solutions. By understanding the potential risks and benefits, we can navigate the AI privacy paradox and ensure the protection of personal information in the AI era.

"Our future success is directly proportional to our ability to understand, adapt to, and integrate new technology into our work." - Sukant Ratnakar

6.5 The Role of Stakeholders in AI and Privacy

In this lesson, we will delve into the role of various stakeholders in maintaining privacy in the realm of Artificial Intelligence (AI). We will identify these key players, understand their responsibilities, and explore how they can help navigate the complex landscape of AI and privacy.

Identifying Key Stakeholders in AI and Privacy

There are several key stakeholders involved in the AI and privacy domain. These include:

- **Government and Regulatory Bodies**: These entities create and enforce laws and regulations related to AI and data privacy.

- **Companies and Organizations**: These entities develop and deploy AI technologies and are responsible for ensuring these technologies respect user privacy.

- **Individual Users**: These are the people who use AI-enabled services and products. They have a right to privacy and a responsibility to understand how their data is used.

- **AI Researchers and Developers**: These are the individuals who design and build AI systems. They have a responsibility to ensure that privacy is considered during the development process.

The Responsibilities of Stakeholders in Protecting Privacy

Each stakeholder has a unique role in protecting privacy in the context of AI:

- **Government and Regulatory Bodies**: They are responsible for creating a legal framework that protects individual privacy rights while enabling innovation in AI. This includes enforcing penalties for privacy breaches and ensuring companies comply with privacy laws.

- **Companies and Organizations**: They must ensure that their AI systems are designed and used in a way that respects privacy. This includes being transparent about how they use customer data and implementing strong data protection measures.

- **Individual Users**: Users need to be aware of their privacy rights and take steps to protect their personal data. This includes understanding privacy policies and adjusting privacy settings on AI-enabled devices and services.

- **AI Researchers and Developers**: They should prioritize privacy when designing and developing AI systems. This includes using techniques like differential privacy to protect individual data.

The Role of Government in Regulating AI and Privacy

Governments play a critical role in regulating AI and privacy. They create laws and regulations that dictate how personal data can be collected, used, and stored. They also enforce these laws, penalizing companies that fail to protect user privacy. In addition, governments can promote privacy-friendly

AI development by funding research into privacy-preserving AI techniques and setting standards for AI and privacy.

The Role of Companies in Ensuring AI and Privacy

Companies are at the forefront of AI development and deployment. They have a responsibility to ensure that their AI systems respect user privacy. This includes being transparent about how they use AI and data, providing users with control over their personal data, and implementing strong data protection measures. Companies can also invest in privacy-preserving AI research and development, creating AI systems that can learn from data without compromising privacy.

In conclusion, each stakeholder plays a vital role in ensuring privacy in the age of AI. By understanding these roles and responsibilities, we can navigate the complex landscape of AI and privacy and ensure that the benefits of AI are realized without compromising our fundamental right to privacy.

"The future depends on what we do in the present." - Mahatma Gandhi

6.6 AI and Privacy: Best Practices

Understanding Best Practices in AI and Privacy

In the age of AI, privacy concerns have come to the forefront. As AI systems become increasingly capable of processing and analyzing vast amounts of data, it's crucial to understand and implement best practices in AI and privacy. These practices ensure that AI systems respect user privacy and comply with data protection laws. They involve principles such as data minimization, purpose limitation, transparency, and user empowerment.

Implementing Privacy by Design in AI Systems

One of the key best practices in AI and privacy is the concept of 'Privacy by Design'. This principle involves integrating privacy considerations into the design and operation of AI systems from the outset, rather than as an afterthought. It includes measures such as:

- **Data Minimization**: Collecting and processing only the minimum amount of data necessary for the AI system to function.

- **Purpose Limitation**: Using the collected data only for the purpose specified at the time of collection.

- **Security Measures**: Implementing robust security measures to protect data from unauthorized access, use, or disclosure.

- **Transparency**: Clearly communicating to users how their data is collected, used, and protected.

- **User Empowerment**: Giving users control over their data, including the ability to access, correct, and delete their data.

Case Study: Successful Implementation of Privacy Measures in AI

Let's look at a case study to understand how these principles can be implemented in practice. A leading tech company, renowned for its AI-powered virtual assistant, has implemented a robust 'Privacy by Design' framework. They collect minimal user data, use it only to improve the functionality of the virtual assistant, and store it securely. They also provide clear and accessible privacy policies, explaining how user data is handled. Users have the ability to review and delete their data at any time. This approach not only ensures compliance with data protection laws but also builds user trust.

Guidelines for Navigating AI and Privacy

Navigating the complex landscape of AI and privacy can be challenging. Here are some guidelines to help:

- **Stay Informed**: Keep up-to-date with the latest developments in AI and privacy, including new laws, regulations, and industry standards.

- **Implement 'Privacy by Design'**: Integrate privacy considerations into the design and operation of your AI systems from the outset.

- **Be Transparent**: Clearly communicate to users how their data is collected, used, and protected.

- **Empower Users**: Give users control over their data, including the ability to access, correct, and delete their data.

- **Ensure Compliance**: Regularly review and update your AI systems to ensure compliance with data protection laws.

By following these best practices, we can harness the power of AI while respecting and protecting user privacy. This approach not only ensures legal compliance but also builds trust, which is essential for the successful adoption and use of AI systems.

"AI's greatest gift is not in answers given, but in questions raised about our own existence." - Dennis Frank

6.7 The Future of AI and Privacy

In this lesson, we will explore the future of AI and privacy. We will discuss how AI is predicted to shape privacy norms, the potential impact of future AI developments on privacy, and how we can prepare for the future of AI and privacy.

Predicting the Future of AI and Privacy

Predicting the future of AI and privacy is a complex task. As AI technology continues to evolve and become more integrated into our daily lives, the privacy concerns associated with it are also likely to increase. The use of AI in data collection and analysis can lead to enhanced privacy protection, but it can also create new privacy risks. For instance, AI can be used to anonymize data, but it can also be used to de-anonymize it. Therefore, the future of AI and privacy will likely involve a delicate balance between leveraging AI for privacy enhancements and managing the privacy risks it poses.

The Role of AI in Shaping Privacy Norms

AI is not only influenced by privacy norms, but it also plays a role in shaping them. As AI becomes more prevalent, it is likely to change our expectations of privacy. For example, as AI systems become more capable of understanding and predicting our behavior, we may become more comfortable with the idea of sharing our data with these systems. On the other hand, as we become more aware of the privacy risks associated with AI, we may demand stronger privacy protections.

Therefore, the role of AI in shaping privacy norms is likely to be dynamic and evolving.

The Impact of Future AI Developments on Privacy

Future developments in AI are likely to have a significant impact on privacy. For example, advances in AI technology could lead to more sophisticated data analysis techniques, which could potentially be used to infringe on privacy. On the other hand, AI could also be used to develop more effective privacy protection tools. For instance, AI could be used to create more secure encryption methods or to detect and prevent data breaches. Therefore, the impact of future AI developments on privacy will likely be multifaceted and complex.

Preparing for the Future of AI and Privacy

Preparing for the future of AI and privacy involves understanding the potential privacy risks associated with AI and taking steps to mitigate these risks. This could involve advocating for stronger privacy laws, developing more secure AI technologies, and educating the public about the privacy implications of AI. It also involves staying informed about the latest developments in AI and privacy, and being prepared to adapt to changes in this rapidly evolving field.

In conclusion, the future of AI and privacy is likely to be complex and dynamic. As AI continues to evolve, it will both shape and be shaped by privacy norms. While future developments in AI could pose new privacy risks, they could also lead to new opportunities for privacy protection. Therefore, it is essential for us to stay informed and prepared for the future of AI and privacy.

6.8 Navigating the AI Privacy Paradox

Understanding the AI Privacy Paradox: A Recap

Before we delve into strategies for navigating the AI privacy paradox, let's recap what this entails. The AI Privacy Paradox refers to the conflict between the benefits of AI and the potential invasion of privacy it represents. While AI systems can offer personalized experiences and improve our lives in many ways, they do so by collecting, analyzing, and learning from vast amounts of personal data. This data collection and usage can potentially infringe on our privacy rights, leading to the paradox.

Strategies for Navigating the AI Privacy Paradox

Navigating the AI Privacy Paradox requires a multifaceted approach, combining regulatory oversight, technological solutions, and individual vigilance.

Regulatory Oversight: Governments and regulatory bodies play a crucial role in setting guidelines and regulations for data privacy. These regulations should provide clear guidelines on what kind of data can be collected, how it should be stored, and how it can be used.

Technological Solutions: Technology itself can be a part of the solution. Techniques like data anonymization and encryption can help protect personal data. Furthermore, privacy-preserving AI techniques, such as differential privacy and federated learning, can help develop AI systems that learn from data without directly accessing it.

Individual Vigilance: As users of AI systems, we also have a role to play. We need to be aware of the privacy settings of the apps and platforms we use and make informed decisions about what data we are comfortable sharing.

The Role of Education and Awareness in Navigating the AI Privacy Paradox

Education and awareness are key to navigating the AI Privacy Paradox. Users need to be educated about the implications of sharing their data and how to protect their privacy. This includes understanding the privacy policies of the platforms they use, and being aware of their rights when it comes to their data.

Furthermore, professionals working in AI should also be educated about the ethical implications of their work. They should be trained to consider privacy implications when designing and developing AI systems.

Conclusion: Embracing AI while Protecting Privacy

The AI Privacy Paradox is a complex issue that does not have a simple solution. However, by combining regulatory oversight, technological solutions, and individual vigilance, we can navigate this paradox. By doing so, we can enjoy the benefits of AI while also protecting our privacy.

Remember, the goal is not to reject AI due to privacy concerns, but to find ways to embrace it responsibly. As we move forward in the AI era, let's strive to strike a balance between technological advancement and privacy protection.

"Understanding AI is not just about grasping code and algorithms; it's about envisioning a future where technology elevates humanity."
- Dennis Frank

7.1 The Intersection of AI and Entertainment

In this lesson, we will explore the fascinating intersection of artificial intelligence (AI) and entertainment. We will delve into the evolution of AI in this industry, its impact on content creation and consumption, and how it's reshaping the way we experience entertainment.

Understanding the Role of AI in the Entertainment Industry

Artificial Intelligence, a term once confined to the realms of science fiction, has now become an integral part of our everyday lives. Its influence extends to various sectors, and the entertainment industry is no exception. AI is playing a transformative role in the way content is created, distributed, and consumed. It's being used to create new music, script films, power recommendation algorithms, and even to predict box office successes. The potential of AI in entertainment is vast and continues to grow as technology evolves.

The Evolution of AI in Entertainment: From Simple Algorithms to Complex AI Systems

The journey of AI in entertainment has been a fascinating one. It started with simple algorithms used to recommend content based on user preferences and has now evolved to complex AI systems capable of creating content.

In the early days, AI was primarily used in recommendation engines. These engines used simple algorithms to suggest songs, movies, or TV shows based on what the user had previously enjoyed. Over time, these algorithms have become increasingly sophisticated, now considering factors like viewing habits, time of day, and even mood to make recommendations.

In recent years, we've seen AI take on more creative roles. AI algorithms are now being used to script films, compose music, and even create art. These developments have opened up new possibilities for content creation, pushing the boundaries of what's possible in entertainment.

The Impact of AI on Content Creation and Consumption

The impact of AI on the entertainment industry is twofold. On the one hand, it's revolutionizing the way content is created. AI algorithms are now capable of creating music, scripting films, and even generating realistic human faces for use in movies and video games. This not only speeds up the content creation process but also opens up new possibilities for creativity.

On the other hand, AI is also transforming the way we consume content. Recommendation algorithms have made it easier than ever to discover new music, films, and TV shows that align with our tastes. Furthermore, AI is being used to create personalized experiences, tailoring content to individual users. This has led to a more engaging and immersive entertainment experience.

In conclusion, the intersection of AI and entertainment is a dynamic space, brimming with potential. As AI continues to evolve, we can expect to see even more innovative uses of this technology in the entertainment industry. Stay tuned for the next lesson, where we will delve deeper into the role of AI in content creation.

"AI is the looking glass through which we see the possibilities of a new world." - Dennis Frank

7.2 AI in Content Creation: A New Era of Creativity

In this lesson, we will explore how AI is transforming the creative process in the entertainment industry, focusing on scriptwriting, music production, and visual effects.

Transforming the Creative Process

Artificial Intelligence is not just a tool for automation; it's a catalyst for creativity. AI algorithms can analyze vast amounts of data, identify patterns, and generate new content based on those patterns. This capability has opened up new possibilities in the entertainment industry, enabling creators to push the boundaries of their craft.

For instance, AI can generate story ideas, suggest plot developments, or even write entire scripts based on data from previously successful movies or TV shows. In music production, AI can compose new melodies, harmonies, or beats based on a database of songs. And in visual effects, AI can create realistic animations, simulate physical phenomena, or generate virtual characters that interact with real actors.

AI in Scriptwriting

In the realm of scriptwriting, AI is making waves. Algorithms can analyze thousands of scripts, learning the common patterns, themes, and structures that make a story engaging.

Using this knowledge, AI can suggest plot twists and character developments and even generate entire scripts.

One such example is the AI named Benjamin, which wrote the script for the short film "Sunspring." Using a database of thousands of sci-fi scripts, Benjamin created a unique, albeit somewhat nonsensical, script that still managed to intrigue audiences.

AI in Music Production

AI is also making its mark in the world of music. Algorithms can analyze a vast array of songs, learning the patterns, rhythms, and structures that make a tune catchy. Using this knowledge, AI can generate new melodies, harmonies, and beats, creating entirely new compositions.

AIVA (Artificial Intelligence Virtual Artist) is an AI that composes music for films, commercials, and video games. It was trained on a database of classical music and can compose original pieces in various styles.

AI in Visual Effects

AI's role in visual effects is equally impressive. By analyzing thousands of images or videos, AI can generate realistic animations, simulate physical phenomena, or even create virtual characters. This technology is particularly useful in creating realistic CGI for movies and video games.

DeepArt, an AI-powered tool, uses a technique called style transfer to apply the visual style of one image to another. This technology has been used in movies to create unique visual effects, such as the painterly look of the film "Loving Vincent."

AI-Driven Content Creation: Case Studies

AI's potential in content creation is not just theoretical. Many companies and creators are already leveraging AI to create unique and engaging content. For instance, Taryn Southern, a YouTuber and musician, used AI to compose her album "I AM AI." The music was entirely generated by AI, with Southern providing the lyrics and vocals.

In the film industry, AI has been used to create trailers. IBM's AI, Watson, created the trailer for the horror film "Morgan." Watson analyzed hundreds of horror movie trailers and used the insights to select the most suspenseful scenes from the film for the trailer.

Conclusion

AI is revolutionizing the creative process in the entertainment industry, opening up new possibilities for creators and offering audiences unique experiences. As AI continues to evolve, we can expect even more innovative and engaging content in the future. However, as with any technology, it's important to consider the ethical implications and strive to use AI in a way that respects creators' rights and audiences' expectations.

In the next lesson, we will explore how AI is changing the way we consume entertainment, focusing on personalization and recommendation systems.

7.3 AI in Content Consumption: Personalization and Recommendation Systems

Introduction

In the realm of entertainment, Artificial Intelligence (AI) has been a game-changer, particularly in the way we consume content. It has made content consumption more personalized, interactive, and engaging. This lesson will delve into the role of AI in content recommendation and personalization, how it's enhancing user experience on entertainment platforms, and the technology that powers these AI-driven recommendation systems.

The Role of AI in Content Recommendation and Personalization

AI has been instrumental in transforming the way we consume content. One of the most prominent areas where AI has made a significant impact is in content recommendation and personalization. AI-powered recommendation systems analyze user behavior, preferences, and interactions to suggest content that aligns with their tastes. This could be anything from recommending a movie on a streaming platform, suggesting a song on a music app, or even proposing a product on an e-commerce site.

AI's ability to analyze vast amounts of data and identify patterns enables it to predict user preferences with remarkable accuracy. This not only enhances the user experience but also increases engagement, as users are more likely to interact with content that resonates with their interests.

Enhancing User Experience in Entertainment Platforms

AI's role in personalizing content consumption has significantly enhanced user experience on entertainment platforms. For instance, streaming platforms like Netflix and Spotify use AI to analyze user behavior and suggest movies, series, or music that users might enjoy. This personalized approach makes the user feel understood and catered to, enhancing their overall experience.

AI also plays a crucial role in content discovery. With the vast amount of content available on digital platforms, finding content that aligns with a user's taste can be overwhelming. AI-powered recommendation systems simplify this process by curating content based on the user's past behavior, preferences, and interactions.

Understanding the Technology Behind AI-Powered Recommendation Systems

AI-powered recommendation systems rely on machine learning algorithms to analyze user data and predict preferences. These algorithms use techniques like collaborative filtering, content-based filtering, or a hybrid approach to make these predictions.

1. **Collaborative Filtering**: This technique analyzes user behavior and interactions to make recommendations. It operates on the assumption that users who agreed in the past will agree in the future. For instance,

if User A and User B both liked the same movies in the past, and User A likes a new movie, the system will recommend that new movie to User B.

2. **Content-Based Filtering**: This technique recommends items by comparing the content of the items and a user profile. The content of each item is represented as a set of descriptors, such as words in the case of text documents.

3. **Hybrid Approach**: Some recommendation systems combine collaborative filtering and content-based filtering to overcome the limitations of both methods and provide more accurate recommendations.

Conclusion

AI has revolutionized content consumption by making it more personalized and interactive. AI-powered recommendation systems have enhanced user experience on entertainment platforms, making content discovery a breeze. As AI continues to evolve, we can expect even more personalized and immersive content consumption experiences in the future.

7.4 AI in Gaming: Revolutionizing Interactive Entertainment

The world of gaming has always been at the forefront of technological innovation, and the advent of AI has only accelerated this trend. From enhancing gameplay to creating immersive virtual and augmented reality experiences, AI is revolutionizing the gaming industry. In this lesson, we will delve into the impact of AI on video game design, the rise of AI-driven VR and AR experiences, and the future prospects of AI in gaming.

The Impact of AI on Video Game Design and Gameplay

AI has become an integral part of modern video game design. It is used to create intelligent and adaptable non-player characters (NPCs), generate dynamic and responsive environments, and even assist in the game design process itself.

NPCs, for instance, are often controlled by AI algorithms, enabling them to react to player actions in a realistic and unpredictable manner. This adds depth and complexity to the game, enhancing the player's immersion and engagement.

AI is also used to create dynamic and responsive game environments. These environments can adapt to player actions, creating a unique and personalized gaming experience. For example, a game might use AI to alter the difficulty level based on the player's skill, or to generate new levels and challenges on the fly.

Furthermore, AI is increasingly being used to assist in the game design process. AI algorithms can generate new game elements, test game mechanics, and even create entire games from scratch. This not only speeds up the game development process but also allows for the creation of more complex and innovative games.

The Rise of AI-Driven Virtual Reality (VR) and Augmented Reality (AR) Experiences

AI is also playing a crucial role in the development of VR and AR technologies. VR and AR games provide immersive experiences that blur the line between the virtual and the real world. AI enhances these experiences by adding a layer of interactivity and realism.

For example, AI can be used to create realistic VR and AR characters that can interact with the player in real-time. These characters can understand and respond to player actions, creating a more engaging and immersive experience.

AI can also be used to analyze player behavior and adapt the VR or AR environment accordingly. This can include changing the game's difficulty level, altering the game's storyline, or even creating new challenges based on the player's actions.

Future Prospects of AI in Gaming

The future of AI in gaming looks incredibly promising. As AI technology continues to advance, we can expect to see even more innovative and immersive gaming experiences.

One exciting prospect is the use of AI to create fully interactive and dynamic game worlds. These worlds could adapt and evolve based on player actions, creating a truly unique and personalized gaming experience.

Another exciting prospect is the use of AI in game design. With AI, game developers could create more complex and innovative games, pushing the boundaries of what is currently possible.

In conclusion, AI is revolutionizing the gaming industry, creating more engaging, immersive, and personalized gaming experiences. As AI technology continues to advance, we can expect to see even more exciting developments in the world of gaming. Whether you're a game developer, a gamer, or just a tech enthusiast, it's an exciting time to be involved in the gaming.

7.5 AI in Film and Television: Changing the Viewing Experience

Now on to the fascinating world of AI in film and television. Artificial Intelligence is not just a concept that exists within the realm of sci-fi movies anymore. It's a reality that's transforming the way we create, distribute, and consume visual media. Let's delve into the details.

The Role of AI in Film and Television Production

AI is revolutionizing the film and television industry at every stage of production, from scriptwriting to post-production.

Scriptwriting: AI algorithms can analyze vast amounts of data from previous successful scripts to generate new ones. These AI-written scripts can provide a solid foundation for human writers to build upon, enhancing creativity and efficiency.

Casting: AI can analyze an actor's past performances and audience reception to predict their suitability for a particular role. This helps in making informed casting decisions.

Filming: AI-powered drones and cameras can capture high-quality footage, reducing the need for human camera operators. AI can also assist in creating realistic CGI and special effects.

Editing: AI can automate the editing process, identifying the best shots and sequences based on predefined criteria. This can significantly reduce the time and effort required in post-production.

How AI is Transforming the Way We Watch and Interact with Visual Media

AI is also changing the viewer's experience in significant ways.

Personalized Recommendations: AI algorithms analyze your viewing history and preferences to recommend content that you are likely to enjoy. This makes content discovery easier and enhances viewer engagement.

Interactive Content: AI enables the creation of interactive content where viewers can influence the storyline. This immersive experience makes viewing more engaging and personalized.

Accessibility: AI-powered tools like automated captioning and audio descriptions make visual media more accessible to people with disabilities.

The Future of AI in Film and Television

The future of AI in film and television looks promising. As AI technology evolves, we can expect more personalized and immersive viewing experiences. AI might also democratize content creation, enabling anyone with a good idea to create high-quality visual content.

AI also raises some challenges. For instance, the ethical implications of AI-written scripts or deepfake technology need to be addressed. As we navigate this exciting AI-driven landscape, it's crucial to balance innovation with ethical considerations.

In conclusion, AI is not just changing the way we watch film and television; it's transforming the entire industry. As we embrace this new creative paradigm, we are witnessing the dawn of a new era in entertainment.

"We cannot always build the future for our youth, but we can build our youth for the future."
- Franklin D. Roosevelt

7.6 AI in Music: The Sound of the Future

Artificial Intelligence is not just transforming industries like healthcare, finance, or retail, it's also making a significant impact on the creative sectors, including music. This lesson will delve into the fascinating world of AI in music, exploring how it's changing music composition, production, and consumption, and what the future holds.

AI in Music Composition and Production

AI is revolutionizing the way music is composed and produced. Traditionally, creating a piece of music required a deep understanding of music theory, creativity, and technical skills. Now, AI is making it possible for anyone to create music, even without any musical background.

AI-powered tools can generate melodies, harmonies, and rhythms based on different music genres, styles, and moods. These tools use machine learning algorithms that have been trained on vast amounts of music data, enabling them to create original compositions that sound like they were created by human musicians.

AI is also being used in music production to automate tasks such as mixing and mastering, which can save time and reduce costs. For instance, AI can analyze a piece of music and automatically adjust the volume levels of different instruments, balance the stereo field, and apply equalization and compression to achieve a polished sound.

AI in Music Discovery and Listening

AI is also changing the way we discover and listen to music. Music streaming platforms like Spotify and Pandora use AI algorithms to analyze our listening habits and preferences, and then recommend songs and artists that we might like. These recommendation systems have made it easier than ever to discover new music that aligns with our tastes.

AI is also being used to create personalized playlists and radio stations, and even to generate music on the fly based on our mood or activity. This level of personalization is enhancing our music listening experience and making it more engaging and enjoyable.

The Future of AI in Music

The use of AI in music is still in its early stages, but the potential is enormous. As AI technology continues to improve, we can expect to see even more sophisticated AI compositions and productions that are indistinguishable from human-created music.

In the future, we might see AI musicians performing live concerts, AI software that can compose a hit song in seconds, or AI music teachers that can provide personalized instruction based on our learning style and progress.

However, the rise of AI in music also raises important ethical and legal questions. Who owns the copyright to a piece of music created by an AI? Can an AI be creative, or is it simply mimicking human creativity? These are complex issues that we will need to navigate as we embrace the AI revolution in music.

In conclusion, AI is transforming the music industry in profound ways, from the way music is composed and produced, to the way we discover and listen to music. As we move into the future, we can look forward to a world where AI and music coexist in harmony, creating new possibilities and experiences for creators and consumers alike.

"The future is something which everyone reaches at the rate of 60 minutes an hour, whatever he does, whoever he is." - C.S. Lewis

7.7 The Ethical Implications of AI in Entertainment

As AI continues to revolutionize the entertainment industry, it also brings with it a host of ethical considerations that we must address. In this lesson, we will explore these ethical implications, focusing on AI's role in content creation and consumption, the debate over AI's role in creativity and originality, and how to navigate the ethical dilemmas of AI in entertainment.

Understanding the Ethical Considerations of AI in Content Creation and Consumption

AI is increasingly being used to create content, from writing scripts to composing music and even creating virtual influencers. While this opens up new possibilities for creativity, it also raises important ethical questions. For instance, who owns the rights to AI-generated content? Is it the developers who created the AI, or is it the AI itself? And what about the consumers? How do we ensure that AI-generated content is transparent and does not manipulate consumers' emotions or behavior in unethical ways?

The Debate Over AI's Role in Creativity and Originality

Another major ethical consideration is the role of AI in creativity and originality. Can AI truly be creative, or is it merely mimicking human creativity? And if AI can create content that is indistinguishable from human-created content, what does that mean for artists and creators? Does it devalue human creativity, or does it push us to be more creative and innovative? These are complex questions with no easy answers, but they are crucial to consider as we navigate the AI revolution in entertainment.

Navigating the Ethical Dilemmas of AI in Entertainment

So, how do we navigate these ethical dilemmas? First, we need to have open and honest conversations about the role of AI in entertainment and the ethical implications it brings. This includes involving all stakeholders, from AI developers and content creators to consumers and policymakers.

Second, we need to establish clear guidelines and regulations for AI in entertainment. This includes issues such as ownership rights to AI-generated content, transparency in AI-generated content, and the ethical use of AI in content creation and consumption.

Finally, we need to educate ourselves and others about AI and its ethical implications. By understanding AI and its potential impacts, we can make informed decisions about its use in entertainment and ensure that it is used in a way that respects our ethical values and principles.

In conclusion, the ethical implications of AI in entertainment are complex and multifaceted, but by understanding these issues and navigating them with care, we can ensure that the

AI revolution in entertainment is not only technologically in-novative but also ethically responsible.

"AI is the bridge between the known and the unknown, leading us to un-charted territories of innovation."
- Dennis Frank

7.8 The Economic Impact of AI in Entertainment

In this lesson, we will explore the economic impact of AI on the entertainment industry. We will delve into how AI is reshaping the financial dynamics of the industry, its role in marketing and distribution, and what the future may hold.

AI Influencing Economic Dynamics

Artificial Intelligence (AI) is significantly influencing the economic dynamics of the entertainment industry. AI technologies such as machine learning, natural language processing, and computer vision are being harnessed to automate tasks, enhance creative processes, and personalize user experiences. This has led to increased efficiency and cost savings, allowing companies to allocate resources more strategically.

AI is also driving new revenue streams. For instance, AI-driven personalization can increase user engagement and retention, leading to higher subscription rates for streaming services. Similarly, AI can enhance in-game experiences in the gaming industry, encouraging players to make in-app purchases.

AI in Entertainment Marketing and Distribution

AI is revolutionizing entertainment marketing and distribution. AI algorithms can analyze vast amounts of data to understand consumer preferences, enabling targeted marketing and personalized recommendations. This not only improves customer satisfaction but also increases the effectiveness of marketing campaigns, leading to higher sales.

In terms of distribution, AI can optimize content delivery based on user behavior and network conditions, ensuring a smooth and high-quality viewing or gaming experience. AI can also help in predicting the success of a movie or a song, aiding in strategic decision-making regarding distribution and promotion.

Future Economic Implications of AI in Entertainment

Looking ahead, the economic implications of AI in entertainment are vast. As AI technologies continue to evolve, they will drive further efficiencies and open new opportunities for monetization. For instance, we could see AI being used to create entirely new forms of entertainment, such as interactive virtual reality experiences, which could generate significant revenue.

However, the rise of AI also poses challenges. As AI automates tasks, there could be job displacements in the industry. There are also concerns about the concentration of power and wealth in the hands of a few tech giants who are leading the AI revolution.

In conclusion, AI is having a profound economic impact on the entertainment industry, influencing everything from production to marketing and distribution. While the future holds exciting possibilities, it is crucial to navigate the challenges and ensure that the benefits of AI are shared equitably.

In the next lesson, we will delve into the AI entertainment landscape, exploring the key players and innovations in the field.

"In the dance of AI with humanity, it's not about leading or following, but harmonizing our steps to create a symphony of progress."
- Dennis Frank

7.9 The AI Entertainment Landscape: Key Players and Innovations

Now let's explore the key players and innovations in the AI entertainment landscape. We will delve into how these industry leaders are leveraging AI to revolutionize entertainment and look at some of the most innovative AI-driven solutions. Finally, we will discuss the future of AI in entertainment, with trends and predictions to watch out for.

Key Players Leveraging AI in the Entertainment Industry

In the entertainment industry, several key players are harnessing the power of AI to redefine the way we create and consume content.

- **Netflix**: Netflix uses AI algorithms to provide personalized recommendations to its users. By analyzing viewing patterns, preferences, and behaviors, Netflix can predict what a user might want to watch next, enhancing user experience and engagement.

- **Spotify**: Similar to Netflix, Spotify uses AI to curate personalized playlists for its users. The AI analyzes listening habits, song preferences, and even the time of day to suggest music that the listener might enjoy.

- **Disney**: Disney uses AI in its animation process. AI algorithms help in creating more realistic animations by studying and mimicking the movements of humans and animals. Disney also uses AI to analyze audience reactions in real-time during test screenings of their movies.

- **Epic Games**: Epic Games, the company behind the popular game Fortnite, uses AI to create more immersive gaming experiences. AI is used to control non-player characters, adjust the game's difficulty level in real-time, and even to create virtual worlds.

Innovative AI-Driven Entertainment Solutions

The use of AI in the entertainment industry has led to the emergence of some truly innovative solutions.

- **AI in Film Production**: AI is being used to streamline the process of film production. From scriptwriting, where AI can predict audience reactions to certain plot points, to post-production, where AI can automate tasks like color correction, the impact of AI is widespread.

- **AI in Music Creation**: Companies like Amper Music and AIVA are using AI to compose music. These AI algorithms can create original music in a variety of genres and moods, which can be used in movies, games, and other forms of entertainment.

- **AI in Virtual Reality**: AI is enhancing the VR experience by making it more interactive and immersive. AI algorithms can understand and react to user actions in real-time, creating a more engaging VR experience.

The Future of AI in Entertainment: Trends and Predictions

As we look towards the future, AI's role in the entertainment industry is expected to grow even further.

- **Personalized Content**: As AI algorithms become more sophisticated, we can expect even more personalized content. This could range from AI-generated music based on our mood to AI-curated TV shows based on our viewing history.

- **Interactive Entertainment**: AI will make entertainment more interactive. In gaming, for example, AI could create adaptive gaming environments that change based on the player's actions.

- **AI in Content Creation**: AI will play a larger role in content creation, from writing scripts to creating visual effects. This could lead to more cost-effective and efficient production processes.

In conclusion, AI is transforming the entertainment landscape, with key players leveraging AI to enhance user experience and create innovative solutions. As we look towards the future, the role of AI in entertainment is set to grow, promising exciting developments in the way we create and consume content.

7.10 Adapting to the AI Revolution in Entertainment

By now, we have a solid understanding of how AI is revolutionizing content creation, consumption, gaming, film, television, and music. Now, we will focus on how we can adapt and thrive in this AI-driven landscape.

Skills and Mindset for the AI-Driven Entertainment Industry

The AI revolution in the entertainment industry requires a new set of skills and a fresh mindset. Creatives and professionals need to understand the basics of AI, machine learning, and data analytics. Familiarity with these technologies can help you understand how AI can enhance your creative process and audience engagement.

Embracing a growth mindset is also crucial. The AI landscape is constantly evolving, and professionals must be open to learning and adapting. Remember, AI is not a threat to creativity but a tool that can enhance it.

Leveraging AI in Your Entertainment Career or Business

AI can be a powerful tool in your entertainment career or business. Here's how you can leverage it:

- **Content Creation**: AI can assist in creating scripts, composing music, and even generating visual art. Embrace these tools to enhance your creative process.

  Audience Engagement: AI-powered recommendation systems can help you understand your audience's preferences and deliver personalized content.

- **Marketing and Distribution**: AI can analyze market trends and consumer behavior, helping you make informed decisions about marketing and distribution.

- **Monetization**: AI can help identify the most effective ways to monetize your content, from subscription models to targeted advertising.

Preparing for the Future of AI in Entertainment

The future of entertainment will be increasingly driven by AI. Here's how you can prepare:

- **Stay Informed**: Keep up with the latest developments in AI and entertainment. Attend seminars, follow thought leaders, and read industry reports.

- **Continuous Learning**: Consider taking courses or certifications in AI, machine learning, or data analytics. This will not only enhance your skillset but also help you understand the AI landscape better.

- **Collaborate**: Collaborate with AI experts, data scientists, and other professionals in the field. This can lead to innovative ideas and solutions.

- **Experiment**: Don't be afraid to experiment with AI in your projects. This hands-on experience is invaluable.

In conclusion, the AI revolution in entertainment is an exciting development that holds immense potential for creators and consumers alike. By developing the right skills, leveraging AI tools, and preparing for the future, we can navigate this landscape successfully and thrive in the AI-driven entertainment industry.

"The journey through AI is one of constant discovery, where each finding is a beacon for future explorations."
- Dennis Frank

8.1 Introduction to AI in Education

In this first lesson of our eighth module, "Educational Evolution: AI as a Learning Partner." In this lesson, we will begin our exploration of the role of Artificial Intelligence (AI) in education and its potential to enhance learning experiences.

Understanding the Role of AI in Education

Artificial Intelligence, or AI, has been making waves in various sectors, and education is no exception. AI refers to the simulation of human intelligence processes by machines, especially computer systems. These processes include learning, reasoning, problem-solving, perception, and language understanding.

In education, AI has the potential to revolutionize the way we teach and learn. It can automate administrative tasks, assist with grading, provide personalized learning experiences, and even act as a learning companion for students. AI can also help identify gaps in learning and teaching, providing valuable insights to educators and policymakers.

Exploring the Potential of AI in Enhancing Learning Experiences

AI's potential to enhance learning experiences is vast. One of the significant ways AI can do this is through personalized learning. AI algorithms can analyze a student's performance, learning style, and preference to create a personalized learning path. This means that each student can learn at their own pace, focusing on areas where they need improvement.

AI can also provide instant feedback, helping students understand where they made mistakes and how to correct them. Furthermore, AI can make learning more engaging through gamification, virtual reality, and other interactive technologies.

The Evolution of AI in the Education System

The use of AI in education is not new, but its role has evolved significantly over the years. Initially, AI was used primarily for administrative tasks such as scheduling and record-keeping. However, as technology advanced, AI's role expanded to include teaching and learning.

Today, AI is used in various ways in the education system. For example, AI-powered tutoring systems can provide personalized instruction to students, while AI-driven assessment tools can grade assignments and exams quickly and accurately. AI can also predict student performance, helping educators identify students who may need additional support.

In the future, we can expect AI to play an even more significant role in education. With advancements in AI technology, we may see AI-powered virtual teachers, AI-driven curriculum development, and more.

In conclusion, AI holds immense potential in transforming the education sector. As we delve deeper into this module, we will explore how AI is reshaping education, from personalized learning to student assessment, curriculum development, and beyond.

In the next lesson we will discuss the AI-driven classroom and its implications for teaching and learning.

"In the future, AI will not just be an interface, but a lens through which we see the world." - Unknown

8.2 The AI-Driven Classroom: A New Learning Environment

The future of education, where Artificial Intelligence (AI) plays a pivotal role in transforming traditional classrooms into dynamic learning environments. In this lesson, we will delve into the concept of AI-driven classrooms, explore how AI is revolutionizing the conventional classroom setting, and discuss various AI tools and applications that are enhancing the learning experience.

The Concept of AI-Driven Classrooms

The AI-driven classroom is a concept that integrates AI technologies into the education system to create a more personalized, interactive, and effective learning experience. This new paradigm shifts away from the traditional 'one-size-fits-all' teaching approach, leveraging AI's capabilities to tailor education to each student's unique learning style, pace, and understanding.

AI-driven classrooms harness the power of AI to analyze vast amounts of data, including students' learning patterns, strengths, weaknesses, and progress, to provide customized learning paths. This data-driven approach enables educators to make informed decisions, optimize teaching strategies, and enhance student engagement and learning outcomes.

How AI is Changing the Traditional Classroom Setting

AI is playing a transformative role in reshaping the traditional classroom setting. Here are a few ways how:

Personalized Learning: AI enables personalized learning by adapting educational content to meet each student's individual needs. It can identify gaps in learning, suggest resources for improvement, and adjust the difficulty level of tasks based on the student's performance.

Automated Administrative Tasks: AI can automate routine administrative tasks such as grading assignments and scheduling classes, freeing up educators' time to focus more on teaching and less on paperwork.

Intelligent Tutoring Systems: AI-powered tutoring systems provide students with personalized tutoring, offering real-time feedback and guidance, and allowing them to learn at their own pace.

Predictive Analytics: AI can predict students' performance and learning outcomes based on their past performance and learning patterns. This information can help educators intervene early and provide necessary support to students who may be at risk of falling behind.

AI Tools and Applications in Classrooms

Several AI tools and applications are being used in classrooms to enhance the learning experience. These include:

AI-Powered Educational Apps: Apps like Socratic and Duolingo use AI to provide personalized learning experiences. They adapt to the learner's pace and understanding, offering customized content and real-time feedback.

Learning Management Systems (LMS): AI-powered LMS like Canvas and Blackboard analyze students' learning patterns to provide personalized learning paths and resources.

Virtual Reality (VR) and Augmented Reality (AR): VR and AR technologies provide immersive learning experiences, making complex concepts easier to understand.

Chatbots: AI-powered chatbots can answer students' queries 24/7, providing instant support and assistance.

In conclusion, the AI-driven classroom is not a distant future concept; it is happening now. AI is revolutionizing the education sector, transforming the way we teach and learn. As we continue to embrace this technology, we can look forward to a more personalized, efficient, and engaging learning experience.

"The best way to predict the future is to invent it." - Alan Kay

8.3 Personalized Learning with AI

The Concept of Personalized Learning

Personalized learning is an educational approach that aims to customize learning for each student's strengths, needs, skills, and interests. It's about tailoring the teaching methods, pace, and content to match each student's learning style and capability. This approach acknowledges that each student is unique and learns differently, and therefore, a one-size-fits-all approach may not be the most effective way to educate.

How AI Enables Personalized Learning

Artificial Intelligence (AI) has the potential to take personalized learning to a whole new level. AI can analyze a vast amount of data about a student's learning behaviors, preferences, and performance in real-time. This data analysis allows AI to identify patterns and trends, which can be used to create a personalized learning path for each student.

For instance, AI can determine if a student learns better through visual aids, text, or audio and can adjust the content delivery accordingly. If a student is struggling with a particular topic, AI can identify this and provide additional resources or change the teaching approach to help the student grasp the concept.

Moreover, AI can adapt the pace of learning based on the student's performance. If a student is quickly grasping concepts, AI can introduce more advanced topics. On the other hand, if a student is struggling, AI can slow down and focus on reinforcing the basics.

Benefits of AI-Driven Personalized Learning

AI-driven personalized learning offers several benefits:

1. **Improved Learning Outcomes**: By tailoring the learning experience to each student's needs, AI can enhance comprehension and retention, leading to improved learning outcomes.

2. **Increased Engagement**: Personalized learning materials that cater to a student's interests and learning style can boost engagement and motivation.

3. **Efficient Learning**: AI can identify and focus on areas where a student needs improvement, making learning more efficient.

4. **Continuous Progress Monitoring**: AI can provide real-time feedback to both students and educators, allowing for continuous progress monitoring and timely interventions.

5. **Flexibility**: AI-driven personalized learning can occur anytime, anywhere, making it a flexible option for students.

In conclusion, AI has the potential to revolutionize personalized learning, making education more effective, engaging, and efficient. As we move forward in the AI era, embracing AI in education will be crucial in preparing students for the future.

8.4 AI and Adaptive Learning Systems

In this lesson, we will delve into the concept of adaptive learning systems and how Artificial Intelligence (AI) plays a pivotal role in their development. We will also explore real-world case studies of successful adaptive learning systems.

Understanding Adaptive Learning Systems

Adaptive learning systems are educational platforms that use technology to modify the presentation of material in response to student performance. Unlike traditional learning methods, which follow a one-size-fits-all approach, adaptive learning systems tailor the learning experience to meet the unique needs of each student. They adjust the pace, level of difficulty, and type of content based on the learner's performance, ensuring a personalized and effective learning experience.

Role of AI in Developing Adaptive Learning Systems

AI is the driving force behind adaptive learning systems. It uses machine learning algorithms to analyze a student's learning patterns, preferences, and performance. Based on this data, AI can predict what type of content the student will benefit from the most and when they might need it.

For example, if a student struggles with a particular concept, the AI can provide additional resources or change the teaching approach to help the student understand better. If a student excels in a certain area, the AI can present more challenging content to keep the student engaged and stimulated.

AI can also provide real-time feedback to both students and educators, highlighting areas of strength and weakness. This allows for timely intervention and support, leading to improved learning outcomes.

Case Studies of Successful Adaptive Learning Systems

Let's look at some successful applications of AI in adaptive learning systems:

1. **Knewton**: Knewton is an adaptive learning technology provider that uses AI to personalize educational content. It analyzes student data to determine how each student learns best and then tailors the content accordingly. Knewton's technology has been adopted by various education providers, demonstrating improved student engagement and learning outcomes.

2. **ALEKS (Assessment and Learning in Knowledge Spaces)**: ALEKS is a web-based, AI-driven assessment and learning system. It uses adaptive questioning to quickly and accurately determine exactly what a student knows and doesn't know in a course. ALEKS then instructs the student on the topics they are most ready to learn.

3. **DreamBox Learning**: DreamBox Learning offers an AI-driven online math learning platform for K-8 students. The platform adapts to the learner's level and helps them master new concepts at their own pace. DreamBox Learning has been shown to improve math scores and boost student confidence.

By leveraging AI, these adaptive learning systems have been able to provide a personalized, engaging, and effective learning experience. They represent the potential of AI in transforming education and enhancing learning outcomes.

In the next lesson, we will explore how AI is used in student assessment and feedback, another critical aspect of the learning process.

"The future starts today, not tomorrow." - Pope John Paul II

8.5 AI in Student Assessment and Feedback

In this lesson, we will explore how Artificial Intelligence (AI) is changing the landscape of student assessment and feedback. AI's ability to analyze data and generate insights is transforming the way educators evaluate student performance and provide feedback.

The Role of AI in Student Assessment

AI is playing a significant role in student assessment by automating the grading process, especially for multiple-choice and fill-in-the-blank tests. AI algorithms can evaluate student responses quickly and accurately, reducing the workload for educators and providing immediate results to students.

Moreover, AI is not limited to grading objective tests. Advanced AI systems can now evaluate subjective responses, such as essays and short-answer questions, by analyzing the semantics and syntax of the student's response. These AI systems can also check for plagiarism, ensuring the originality of the student's work.

AI also enables adaptive testing, where the difficulty of the test adjusts based on the student's performance. This method provides a more accurate measure of a student's knowledge and skills.

How AI Provides Real-Time Feedback to Students

One of the most significant advantages of using AI in education is the ability to provide real-time, personalized feedback to students. AI systems can analyze a student's response immediately after submission, identify errors, and provide corrective feedback. This immediate feedback helps students understand their mistakes and learn from them right away, enhancing their learning experience.

AI can also provide personalized feedback based on a student's learning style and progress. For example, if a student is struggling with a particular concept, the AI system can provide additional resources or exercises to help the student master that concept.

The Impact of AI-Driven Assessments on Student Performance

AI-driven assessments and feedback can significantly improve student performance. The immediate and personalized feedback helps students identify their strengths and weaknesses, focus on areas that need improvement, and learn at their own pace.

Moreover, AI-driven assessments provide a more accurate measure of a student's knowledge and skills, as they consider the student's performance over time, not just a single test. This comprehensive evaluation can help educators develop more effective teaching strategies and improve the overall quality of education.

In conclusion, AI is revolutionizing student assessment and feedback, making them more efficient, personalized, and impactful. As AI continues to evolve, we can expect even more significant transformations in the education sector.

8.6 AI in Curriculum Development and Course Design

Introduction

In this lesson, we will explore the transformative role of Artificial Intelligence (AI) in curriculum development and course design. As we delve into this topic, we will understand how AI is not only changing the way we teach but also how we design and develop educational content.

Understanding how AI aids in Curriculum Development

Curriculum development is a critical aspect of education that determines what students learn, how they learn it, and how their learning is assessed. Traditionally, this has been a labor-intensive process requiring educators to manually analyze educational standards, student data, and learning outcomes.

AI is revolutionizing this process by automating the analysis of vast amounts of data to inform curriculum development. With AI, we can now analyze student performance data in real-time, identify learning gaps, and adapt the curriculum to meet the unique needs of each student. AI can also predict future learning outcomes based on current data, allowing educators to proactively modify the curriculum to enhance student success.

The Role of AI in Course Design

Course design is another area where AI is making significant strides. In traditional course design, educators often rely on their experience and intuition to create course content, structure lessons, and develop assessments. This approach, while valuable, can be time-consuming and may not always meet the diverse learning needs of all students.

AI can assist in course design by analyzing student data to understand their learning styles, preferences, and performance. This data can then be used to design personalized courses that cater to each student's unique learning needs. For instance, if a student learns best through visual content, AI can recommend incorporating more videos and infographics into the course.

AI can also automate the creation of assessments, generating questions based on the course content and adjusting the difficulty level based on the student's performance. This ensures that assessments are not only aligned with the course content but also appropriately challenging for each student.

The Potential of AI in Creating Dynamic and Interactive Courses

One of the most exciting potentials of AI in education is its ability to create dynamic and interactive courses. Instead of static course content, AI can create interactive lessons that adapt in real-time based on the student's performance.

For example, if a student is struggling with a particular concept, the AI can automatically provide additional resources or change the teaching approach to help the student understand. Conversely, if a student is excelling, the AI can introduce more advanced content to keep the student challenged and engaged.

Moreover, AI can incorporate gamification elements into the course, turning learning into a fun and engaging experience. This not only enhances student engagement but also promotes active learning, where students are actively involved in their learning process.

Conclusion

In conclusion, AI is transforming curriculum development and course design, making it more data-driven, personalized, and dynamic. As we continue to harness the power of AI in education, we can look forward to more effective and engaging learning experiences that cater to the unique needs of each student. This is just the beginning of the AI revolution in education, and the future holds even more exciting possibilities.

"The future is not an inheritance, it is an opportunity and an obligation."
- Bill Clinton

8.7 AI and Special Education

Introduction

Artificial Intelligence (AI) has emerged as a game-changer in the field of education, and its potential in special education is particularly noteworthy. It offers promising possibilities for catering to diverse learning needs and creating inclusive learning environments. In this lesson, we will delve into the role of AI in special education, explore how it can help meet diverse learning needs, and examine real-world applications through case studies.

The Potential of AI in Special Education

AI has the potential to revolutionize special education by providing personalized learning experiences tailored to the unique needs of each student. It can help overcome traditional barriers in special education, such as limited resources and lack of individualized attention.

AI-powered tools can provide adaptive learning environments that adjust to the learner's pace and level of understanding. They can also provide real-time feedback, helping educators to monitor progress and intervene when necessary. Furthermore, AI can help in creating engaging, multi-sensory learning experiences that can significantly aid students with special needs.

Catering to Diverse Learning Needs

One of the key advantages of AI in special education is its ability to cater to diverse learning needs. AI can help create personalized learning paths, taking into account the learner's strengths, weaknesses, interests, and learning style.

For instance, AI can help students with dyslexia by providing text-to-speech and speech-to-text features, making reading and writing more accessible. For students with autism, AI can help in developing social and communication skills through interactive games and activities.

Moreover, AI can help students with physical disabilities by providing assistive technologies, such as voice-activated controls and eye-tracking software, making digital learning resources more accessible.

Case Studies of AI Applications in Special Education

Let's explore some real-world applications of AI in special education through these case studies:

1. **Otsimo**: Otsimo is an AI-powered app designed to provide personalized education for children with special needs. It offers a range of games and activities designed to improve various skills, such as motor skills, cognitive skills, and language skills. The app uses machine learning algorithms to adapt to the child's learning pace and provides real-time feedback to parents and educators.

2. **Brain Power**: Brain Power is a company that leverages AI to help children with autism improve their social and communication skills. They have developed a wearable device that uses AI to provide real-time coaching during social interactions. The device

can recognize and interpret social cues, helping the child to understand and respond appropriately.

3. **Microsoft's Learning Tools**: Microsoft has developed a set of free learning tools that leverage AI to make classroom activities more accessible for students with special needs. These tools include Immersive Reader, which provides text-to-speech, speech-to-text, and other features to aid reading and writing.

Conclusion

AI holds immense potential in transforming special education by providing personalized, adaptive, and inclusive learning experiences. As AI continues to evolve, it promises to bring about significant improvements in the way we cater to diverse learning needs, making education more accessible for all.

In the next lesson, we will explore the role of AI in education administration.

8.8 AI in Education Administration

Introduction

In the modern world, Artificial Intelligence (AI) is not just a buzzword. It's a technology that's transforming industries and sectors, and education is no exception. One of the areas in education where AI has shown significant potential is in administration. In this lesson, we will explore the role of AI in education administration, how it can streamline administrative tasks, and its impact on decision-making.

The Role of AI in Education Administration

Educational administration involves a wide range of tasks, from scheduling and planning to record-keeping and reporting. AI has the potential to automate many of these tasks, making them more efficient and less prone to human error.

For instance, AI-powered systems can automate the process of scheduling classes and exams, considering factors such as room availability, teacher availability, and student preferences. This not only saves time but also ensures optimal utilization of resources.

AI can also help in record-keeping and reporting. AI-powered systems can automatically track student attendance, grades, and other data, and generate reports in real-time. This not only reduces the workload for administrators but also provides them with up-to-date information at their fingertips.

Streamlining Administrative Tasks with AI

AI can streamline administrative tasks in several ways. For instance, AI-powered chatbots can handle routine inquiries from students and parents, freeing up time for administrators to focus on more complex tasks.

AI can also automate the process of grading assignments and exams. This not only saves time for teachers but also ensures consistency and fairness in grading.

Moreover, AI can help in managing school finances. AI-powered systems can track income and expenses, generate financial reports, and even predict future financial trends. This can help administrators make informed decisions about budgeting and resource allocation.

AI and Decision-Making in Education Administration

AI can play a crucial role in decision-making in education administration. By analyzing large amounts of data, AI can provide insights that can help administrators make informed decisions.

For instance, AI can analyze student performance data to identify patterns and trends. This can help administrators identify students who are struggling and need additional support, or subjects that are particularly challenging for students.

AI can also analyze data on school performance, such as test scores and graduation rates, to identify areas for improvement. This can help administrators make decisions about curriculum development, teacher training, and other strategic initiatives.

Moreover, AI can predict future trends based on historical data. This can help administrators plan for the future, whether it's expanding the school, hiring new teachers, or introducing new programs.

Conclusion

In conclusion, AI has the potential to revolutionize education administration. By automating routine tasks, providing real-time data, and supporting decision-making, AI can make education administration more efficient, effective, and forward-looking. As we embrace the AI revolution, it's crucial for education administrators to understand and leverage the potential of AI. In the next lesson, we will explore the ethical considerations of AI in education.

"AI's true potential lies in its ability to transform the ordinary into the extraordinary." - Dennis Frank

8.9 The Ethical Considerations of AI in Education

Understanding the Ethical Implications of AI in Education

Artificial Intelligence (AI) holds immense potential for revolutionizing the education sector. However, with this potential comes a set of ethical considerations that educators, administrators, and policymakers must address.

AI systems in education, like any other sector, operate based on the data they are fed. This data often includes sensitive information about students, such as their learning styles, strengths, weaknesses, personal interests, and even behavioral patterns. While this data can be used to personalize learning and improve educational outcomes, it also raises ethical concerns related to privacy, consent, and data security.

Moreover, AI systems, depending on their design and implementation, may inadvertently introduce or perpetuate biases. For instance, an AI system might favor students from certain backgrounds or with certain learning styles, thereby creating a skewed learning environment.

Privacy Concerns Related to AI in Education

One of the most significant ethical concerns with the use of AI in education is the privacy of student data. AI systems require vast amounts of data to function effectively, and in the context of education, this data is often personal and sensitive.

The use of AI in education necessitates the collection, storage, and processing of student data, raising concerns about who has access to this data, how it is used, and how it is protected. There is also the question of consent - are students and their parents fully informed about how their data is being used? Are they given an option to opt-out?

These concerns highlight the need for stringent data protection policies and practices in educational institutions that use AI. It also underscores the importance of transparency in how AI systems operate and use data.

Strategies for Ethical Decision-Making in AI-Driven Education

Addressing the ethical implications of AI in education requires a multi-faceted approach. Here are a few strategies:

Transparency: AI systems should be transparent in their operations. Students, parents, and educators should understand how these systems use data and make decisions.

Informed Consent: Before collecting and using student data, educational institutions should obtain informed consent from students and their parents. This involves explaining in clear, understandable terms how the data will be used and giving them the option to opt out.

Data Protection: Educational institutions should have robust data protection measures in place. This includes secure data storage, limited data access, and regular data audits.

Bias Mitigation: AI systems should be designed and implemented in a way that minimizes bias. This might involve using diverse training data, regularly reviewing and updating algorithms, and incorporating feedback from students and educators.

Ethics Training: Educators and administrators should receive training on the ethical implications of AI. This can help them make informed decisions about the use of AI in their classrooms and institutions.

In conclusion, while AI holds great promise for enhancing education, it is crucial to navigate its ethical implications carefully. By prioritizing transparency, informed consent, data protection, bias mitigation, and ethics training, we can harness the benefits of AI in education while minimizing potential risks.

8.10 The Future of AI in Education

As we come to the end of this module, it's time to look ahead and explore the future of AI in education. AI is not just a fleeting trend; it's a transformative force that is reshaping the education sector. Let's delve into what the future might hold.

Predicting the Future Trends of AI in Education

AI is poised to become an integral part of the education system. Here are some predicted trends:

1. **Personalized Learning**: AI algorithms will become more sophisticated, enabling more personalized and adaptive learning experiences. These systems will be able to analyze a student's learning style, pace, and areas of difficulty to provide tailored educational content.

2. **Intelligent Tutoring Systems**: These systems will evolve to provide more comprehensive support, offering detailed feedback and explanations just like a human tutor. They will be able to assist students in a wide range of subjects, making education more accessible.

3. **AI-Driven Content Creation**: AI will play a significant role in content creation, generating educational

materials like textbooks, quizzes, and interactive lessons. This will allow for the rapid creation of up-to-date educational content.

4. **Data-Driven Insights**: AI will enable educators to gain deeper insights into student performance and learning gaps. This will facilitate more effective teaching strategies and interventions.

The Role of AI in Shaping the Future of Education

AI is set to revolutionize education in several ways:

1. **Democratizing Education**: AI can make quality education accessible to all, regardless of geographical location or socio-economic status. Virtual tutors and AI-driven educational platforms can reach students in remote areas, bridging the educational divide.

2. **Enhancing Learning Experience**: AI can make learning more engaging and interactive. From virtual reality experiences to gamified learning platforms, AI can transform the way students learn.

3. **Improving Efficiency**: AI can automate administrative tasks, freeing up time for educators to focus on teaching. It can also streamline the grading process, providing instant feedback to students.

Preparing for the Future: Adapting to an AI-Driven Education System

As we move towards an AI-driven education system, it's crucial to adapt and prepare for this change. Here are some ways to do so:

1. **Embrace Lifelong Learning**: As AI continues to evolve, the need for continuous learning becomes more important. Stay updated with the latest AI trends and applications in education.

2. **Develop Digital Literacy**: As AI becomes more prevalent, digital literacy becomes a crucial skill. Understand the basics of AI and how it works in the context of education.

3. **Promote Ethical Use of AI**: As we leverage AI in education, it's important to consider the ethical implications. Promote transparency, fairness, and privacy in the use of AI.

In conclusion, the future of AI in education holds immense potential. As we embrace this AI-driven era, it's essential to harness its benefits responsibly and ethically while preparing for the challenges it may bring. Let's look forward to a future where AI and education work hand in hand to create enriching learning experiences.

9.1 Understanding Ethical AI

Welcome to the first lesson in our module on Ethical AI. In this lesson, we will introduce the concept of ethical AI, discuss its importance, explore some common ethical issues in AI, and delve into a few case studies that highlight these ethical dilemmas.

Introduction to Ethical AI

Artificial Intelligence (AI) has become an integral part of our lives, influencing everything from our shopping habits to our healthcare. But as AI continues to evolve and become more sophisticated, it's crucial that we consider the ethical implications of these technologies.

Ethical AI refers to the practice of developing and using AI in a way that aligns with our moral values and societal norms. It involves ensuring fairness, transparency, privacy, and accountability in AI systems.

Importance of Ethics in AI

Ethics in AI is not just a theoretical concept, but a practical necessity. As AI systems make more decisions that affect individuals and society, it's important that these decisions are made ethically.

Ethical considerations help prevent bias and discrimination in AI systems, protect user privacy, and ensure that AI is used for the benefit of all, not just a select few. They also help to build trust in AI systems, which is crucial for their widespread adoption and use.

Common Ethical Issues in AI

There are several common ethical issues that arise in the field of AI. One of the most prevalent is bias. AI systems learn from data, and if that data is biased, the AI system will likely be biased too. This can lead to discriminatory practices, such as racial or gender bias in hiring algorithms.

Privacy is another major ethical concern. AI systems often require large amounts of personal data to function effectively, which can lead to privacy violations if not handled correctly.

Finally, there's the issue of accountability. If an AI system makes a decision that has negative consequences, who is responsible? The developer of the AI system? The user? These are complex questions that we are still grappling with.

Case Studies Highlighting Ethical Dilemmas in AI

To better understand these ethical issues, let's look at a few real-world case studies.

One example is the use of facial recognition technology. While it can be used for beneficial purposes, such as finding missing persons, it can also be used for surveillance and profiling, raising serious ethical concerns.

Another example is the use of AI in hiring. Some companies use AI to screen resumes and predict job performance. But these algorithms can be biased, leading to unfair hiring practices.

In the next lessons, we will delve deeper into these ethical issues and discuss strategies for ethical decision-making in AI. But for now, it's important to understand that ethical AI is not just about preventing harm, but about actively promoting fairness, transparency, privacy, and accountability.

In the world of AI, ethics is not an afterthought, but a fundamental part of the design and implementation process. As we continue to navigate the AI landscape, it's crucial that we keep these ethical considerations at the forefront of our minds.

"For the wise, the future is not an unknown destination but a creation of one's own imagination." - Unknown

9.2 The Moral Dimensions of AI

In this lesson, we will explore the moral dimensions of Artificial Intelligence (AI). We will delve into the implications of AI decision-making, discuss AI's role in human rights, social justice, inequality, and its impact on privacy and security.

The Moral Implications of AI Decision-Making

AI systems, with their ability to analyze vast amounts of data and make decisions in real-time, are increasingly being used in areas that have significant moral implications. These include healthcare, finance, criminal justice, and even autonomous vehicles.

For instance, an AI system might be tasked with deciding which patient should receive a life-saving treatment when resources are limited, or who should get parole in a criminal justice setting. These decisions have profound moral implications and raise questions about the fairness and transparency of AI decision-making.

AI and Human Rights: A Discussion

AI has the potential to both uphold and violate human rights. On the one hand, AI can be used to detect human rights abuses, such as identifying instances of hate speech or violence in social media posts. On the other hand, AI systems can also be used in ways that infringe on human rights, such as surveillance technologies that invade privacy or AI algorithms that perpetuate discrimination.

It's crucial to ensure that AI technologies are developed and used in ways that respect human rights. This requires a thorough understanding of human rights principles and a commitment to embedding these principles into AI systems.

The Role of AI in Social Justice and Inequality

AI can both exacerbate and alleviate social justice issues and inequality. For example, AI systems can perpetuate bias and discrimination if they're trained on biased data. This can lead to unfair outcomes in areas like hiring, lending, and law enforcement.

Conversely, AI can also be used to promote social justice. For instance, AI can help identify patterns of discrimination or bias, and it can be used to ensure resources are distributed more equitably.

The Impact of AI on Privacy and Security

AI has significant implications for privacy and security. AI technologies like facial recognition and data analytics can invade privacy by collecting and analyzing personal data on a massive scale. At the same time, AI can also be used to enhance security, such as through improved cybersecurity systems that can detect and respond to threats more quickly and accurately.

However, the use of AI for security purposes also raises moral questions. For example, is it ethical to use AI surveillance technologies in public spaces, potentially infringing on people's privacy, in the name of security?

In conclusion, the moral dimensions of AI are complex and multifaceted. As we continue to develop and deploy AI systems, it's crucial to consider these moral implications and strive for an ethical approach to AI.

"In the symphony of the future, AI is not just an instrument; it's a composer creating new melodies of progress."
- Dennis Frank

9.3 Ethical Decision-Making in AI

In this lesson, we will focus on ethical decision-making in AI. We will explore the principles of ethical decision-making, discuss a few ethical frameworks for AI, and delve into the importance of transparency and accountability in AI ethics. We will also examine some case studies to better understand how ethical decisions are made in real-world AI scenarios.

Principles of Ethical Decision-Making in AI

Ethical decision-making in AI revolves around a set of guiding principles that help ensure AI systems are used responsibly and ethically. These principles generally include:

1. **Respect for Autonomy**: AI should respect individuals' ability to make decisions for themselves and not unduly influence or coerce them.

2. **Beneficence**: AI should be used to contribute positively to human welfare and well-being.

3. **Non-Maleficence**: AI should not cause harm to individuals or society.

4. **Justice**: AI should be fair and not lead to discrimination or bias.

5. **Transparency**: AI algorithms and their decision-making processes should be transparent and understandable.

6. **Accountability**: Those who design and deploy AI systems should be held accountable for their outcomes.

Ethical Frameworks for AI: An Overview

Ethical frameworks provide structured approaches to ethical decision-making in AI. They help in identifying ethical issues, analyzing potential impacts, and making informed decisions. Here are a few commonly used ethical frameworks in AI:

1. **Consequentialism**: This framework focuses on the outcomes of an action. In AI, it would involve evaluating the potential benefits and harms of deploying an AI system.

2. **Deontological Ethics**: This approach emphasizes duties and rules. In the context of AI, it would involve adhering to certain ethical rules or guidelines, regardless of the outcome.

3. **Virtue Ethics**: This framework focuses on the character and virtues of the decision-maker. In AI, it would involve considering the virtues of those designing and deploying the AI system.

The Role of Transparency and Accountability in AI Ethics

Transparency and accountability are critical in AI ethics. Transparency involves making the workings of an AI system understandable to its users and stakeholders. It helps build trust in the system and allows for better scrutiny of its decisions.

Accountability, on the other hand, involves holding those responsible for the AI system accountable for its outcomes. It ensures that if an AI system causes harm, those responsible can be held to account, which in turn encourages the responsible design and use of AI.

Case Studies on Ethical Decision-Making in AI

Let's look at a couple of case studies to understand how ethical decision-making works in practice in AI:

1. **Case Study 1 - AI in Healthcare**: An AI system is developed to help doctors diagnose diseases. However, the system sometimes makes mistakes that could potentially harm patients. Here, the principles of non-maleficence and beneficence come into play. The developers need to weigh the benefits of the system (helping diagnose diseases) against the potential harm (misdiagnosis). They also need to ensure transparency (making the workings of the system clear to doctors) and accountability (taking responsibility for mistakes).

2. **Case Study 2 - AI in Hiring**: A company uses an AI system to screen job applicants. However, the system is found to be biased against certain groups. Here, the principles of justice and respect for autonomy are crucial. The company needs to ensure the system is fair and does not infringe on individuals' rights to equal opportunity. It also needs to ensure transparency (making the workings of the system clear to applicants) and accountability (taking responsibility for the bias).

In conclusion, ethical decision-making in AI is a complex process that requires careful consideration of various ethical principles and frameworks. It also necessitates transparency and accountability to ensure responsible and ethical use of AI. As we continue to integrate AI into our lives, understanding and practicing ethical decision-making in AI becomes increasingly important.

"In the hands of the wise, AI is a tool for building a future that respects and enhances human dignity." - Dennis Frank

9.4 AI Bias and Discrimination

Understanding AI Bias and Its Implications

AI bias refers to the systematic and repeatable errors in a computer system that create unfair outcomes, such as privileging one arbitrary group of users over others. It's a phenomenon that occurs when an algorithm produces results that are systematically prejudiced due to erroneous assumptions in the machine learning process.

AI bias can occur due to various reasons, such as:

- **Data Bias**: If the data used to train an AI system is biased, the system will also be biased. For example, if a facial recognition system is trained mostly on images of light-skinned people, it may not perform well on images of dark-skinned people.

- **Algorithmic Bias**: This occurs when the algorithm used to make decisions or predictions is biased, leading to unfair outcomes.

The implications of AI bias are far-reaching. It can lead to discrimination in many areas, including hiring, lending, law enforcement, and healthcare. For example, an AI system used for hiring might be biased against certain demographic groups if the data it was trained on reflected such bias.

The Impact of AI Bias on Society and Individuals

AI bias can have significant impacts on both society and individuals. It can perpetuate existing social inequalities and create new ones. For instance, if an AI system used in hiring is biased against women, it could lead to fewer job opportunities for women and widen the gender gap in employment.

On an individual level, AI bias can lead to unfair treatment. For example, a person might be wrongly flagged as a potential criminal by a biased AI system used in law enforcement.

Strategies to Mitigate AI Bias

Mitigating AI bias is crucial to ensure fairness and justice in AI systems. Here are some strategies to address AI bias:

- **Diversify the Training Data**: Ensuring that the data used to train AI systems is diverse and representative can help reduce data bias.

- **Bias Auditing**: Regularly auditing AI systems for bias can help identify and correct bias. Various tools and techniques are available for bias auditing.

- **Transparency**: Making the workings of AI systems transparent can help identify bias. This includes transparency in the data used, the algorithms applied, and the decision-making process.

- **Inclusion**: Including people from diverse backgrounds in the development and auditing of AI systems can help ensure different perspectives are considered, which can help identify and reduce bias.

Case Studies on AI Bias and Discrimination

There have been several high-profile cases of AI bias and discrimination. For example, a study found that an AI system used by a major healthcare provider was biased against black patients. The system was less likely to refer black patients to programs that aim to improve care for patients with complex medical needs, even when they were sicker than white patients.

In another case, a facial recognition system incorrectly identified 28 members of the U.S. Congress as criminals. The system was found to be less accurate for people with darker skin tones.

These cases highlight the importance of addressing AI bias to ensure fairness and justice in AI systems.

In conclusion, while AI holds great promise, it's crucial to navigate the moral maze of AI bias and discrimination. By understanding and addressing AI bias, we can help ensure that AI systems are fair and just, benefiting all members of society.

9.5 AI, Ethics, and the Law

In this lesson, we will delve into the complex interplay between AI, ethics, and the law. We will explore the legal implications of AI ethics, examine AI and data privacy laws, discuss the role of regulation in promoting ethical AI, and review case studies on legal disputes involving AI ethics.

Legal Implications of AI Ethics

Artificial Intelligence, while being a powerful tool, also presents a myriad of ethical challenges. These challenges have legal implications, as laws are often the tangible expressions of our ethical values. When AI systems make decisions or take actions that have real-world consequences, who is legally responsible? Is it the developers who coded the AI, the users who operate it, or the AI itself? These are some of the questions that lawmakers and legal scholars are grappling with as they try to navigate the legal implications of AI ethics.

AI and Data Privacy Laws

Data is the lifeblood of AI. AI systems need vast amounts of data to learn and make accurate predictions. However, this voracious appetite for data raises serious privacy concerns. Different jurisdictions have enacted data privacy laws to protect individuals' personal information. For instance, the European Union's General Data Protection Regulation (GDPR) has strict rules about how personal data can be collected, stored, processed, and shared. In the context of AI, these laws have significant implications for how AI systems are designed and used.

The Role of Regulation in Promoting Ethical AI

Regulation plays a crucial role in promoting ethical AI. Regulatory bodies can set standards and guidelines for AI development and use, ensuring that AI systems are designed and used ethically. For instance, they can mandate transparency in AI decision-making processes, require audits of AI systems to detect and mitigate bias, and enforce penalties for misuse of AI. However, regulating AI is a complex task that requires a deep understanding of AI technologies and their societal implications.

Case Studies on Legal Disputes Involving AI Ethics

There have been several legal disputes involving AI ethics, and these cases can provide valuable insights into the legal challenges posed by AI. For instance, a case in the United States involved an AI system used in criminal sentencing. The system was accused of being biased against certain racial groups, raising questions about the legality of using such systems in the justice system. In another case, a self-driving car was involved in a fatal accident, leading to a heated debate about who should be held legally responsible - the car's manufacturer, the software developer, or the car itself.

In conclusion, the intersection of AI, ethics, and the law is a complex and rapidly evolving area. As AI continues to permeate our lives, it is crucial that we develop robust legal frameworks that can ensure the ethical use of AI while also fostering innovation. In the next lesson, we will delve deeper into the role of stakeholders in AI ethics.

9.6 The Role of Stakeholders in AI Ethics

The ethical implications of AI are vast and complex, touching on issues of privacy, fairness, accountability, and transparency. To navigate these challenges, it's essential to understand the role of various stakeholders in AI ethics. These stakeholders include AI developers, users, government and regulatory bodies, and the public.

Understanding the Role of Different Stakeholders in AI Ethics

AI ethics is a shared responsibility, and every stakeholder plays a critical role in ensuring that AI is developed and used ethically. Let's explore the roles of these key stakeholders.

AI Developers

AI developers are at the forefront of creating AI systems. They have a significant responsibility to ensure that the AI they develop is ethical. This includes designing AI systems that respect privacy, are transparent in their operations, and do not discriminate against certain groups. Developers should also consider the potential misuse of their AI systems and take steps to prevent such misuse.

AI Users

AI users, whether they are individuals, businesses, or other entities, also have a crucial role in AI ethics. They are responsible for using AI in a way that respects ethical principles. This includes using AI responsibly, respecting the privacy and rights of others when using AI, and being aware of the potential biases and limitations of AI systems.

Government and Regulatory Bodies

Government and regulatory bodies play a critical role in setting the rules and standards for AI ethics. They are responsible for creating laws and regulations that ensure AI is developed and used ethically. This includes regulations that protect privacy, prevent discrimination, and ensure accountability in AI. These bodies also have a role in enforcing these regulations and taking action against those who violate them.

The Public

The public plays a vital role in shaping AI ethics. As the ultimate beneficiaries or victims of AI, the public has a right to be involved in discussions about AI ethics. This includes voicing concerns about AI, participating in public consultations on AI regulations, and advocating for ethical AI practices.

Conclusion

In conclusion, AI ethics is a shared responsibility that involves various stakeholders. Each stakeholder has a unique role and responsibility in ensuring that AI is developed and used ethically. By understanding these roles, we can better navigate the ethical challenges of AI and work towards a future where AI benefits all of humanity.

9.7 Ethical AI in Practice

In this lesson, we will delve into the practical aspects of implementing ethical AI in organizations. We will explore the strategies, roles, case studies, and future prospects of ethical AI.

Strategies for Implementing Ethical AI in Organizations

Implementing ethical AI in an organization is a multi-faceted process. It starts with a clear understanding of what ethical AI means and how it aligns with the organization's values and goals. Once this foundation is laid, the organization can then develop a strategy that includes the following steps:

1. **Policy Development**: Create a comprehensive AI ethics policy that outlines the organization's commitment to ethical AI practices. This policy should address issues such as transparency, fairness, privacy, and accountability.

2. **Training**: Provide training to all employees, not just those directly involved in AI projects, to ensure they understand the ethical implications of AI.

3. **Ethical Design**: Incorporate ethical considerations into the design and development process of AI systems. This includes using fair and unbiased data,

ensuring transparency in AI decision-making, and building systems that respect user privacy.

4. **Monitoring and Evaluation**: Regularly monitor and evaluate AI systems to ensure they are operating ethically. This includes auditing algorithms for bias and conducting impact assessments to identify any potential ethical issues.

The Role of Ethics Committees and AI Ethics Officers

To ensure the effective implementation of ethical AI, many organizations are establishing ethics committees and appointing AI ethics officers.

Ethics Committees: These committees are typically comprised of a diverse group of stakeholders, including representatives from different departments, external experts, and sometimes even customers or users. The committee's role is to provide oversight, guidance, and accountability for the organization's AI ethics strategy.

AI Ethics Officers: An AI Ethics Officer is a relatively new role that is becoming increasingly important as organizations grapple with the ethical implications of AI. The officer's role is to ensure that AI systems are designed, developed, and used in a manner that respects ethical principles.

Case Studies on Organizations Implementing Ethical AI

Several organizations are leading the way in implementing ethical AI. For instance, Google's AI Ethics Committee oversees the company's AI projects to ensure they align with its AI Principles. Similarly, IBM has established the AI Ethics

Board, which provides guidance on AI ethics issues and reviews high-risk AI projects.

The Future of Ethical AI: Challenges and Opportunities

Looking ahead, the future of ethical AI presents both challenges and opportunities. On the one hand, as AI systems become more complex and pervasive, the ethical issues they raise will likely become more complex as well. On the other hand, these challenges present opportunities for organizations to distinguish themselves by demonstrating a strong commitment to ethical AI.

In conclusion, implementing ethical AI is not a one-time task but an ongoing process that requires commitment, vigilance, and a willingness to adapt and learn. As we navigate the AI landscape, it is crucial that we keep ethical considerations at the forefront, not just to avoid potential pitfalls, but to ensure that AI is used in a way that benefits all of society.

"AI will not replace human intelligence; it will enhance it, challenging us to evolve and redefine what it means to be intelligent." - Dennis Frank

9.8 Navigating the Ethical AI Landscape

As we delve deeper into the realm of Artificial Intelligence, we must also navigate the complex landscape of ethical AI. This involves understanding the tools and resources available, the importance of ethics training and education, and the crucial role of ethical leadership in AI.

Tools and Resources for Navigating Ethical AI

There are numerous tools and resources available to help navigate the ethical AI landscape. These include ethical AI guidelines, frameworks, and checklists developed by organizations such as the IEEE, the European Commission, and the Partnership on AI.

These tools provide guidance on key ethical considerations in AI, such as fairness, transparency, privacy, and accountability. They also offer practical advice on how to implement ethical AI in practice, such as conducting impact assessments, testing for bias, and setting up ethics review boards.

The Role of Ethics Training and Education in AI

Ethics training and education play a crucial role in navigating the ethical AI landscape. It's essential for those involved in the design, development, and deployment of AI systems to have a solid understanding of the ethical implications of their work.

This involves not only technical training but also education in areas such as philosophy, law, and social sciences. It's about fostering a multidisciplinary approach to AI, where technologists work alongside ethicists, lawyers, and social scientists to ensure that AI is developed and used in a way that respects our ethical values and norms.

The Importance of Ethical Leadership in AI

Ethical leadership is paramount in navigating the ethical AI landscape. Leaders play a crucial role in setting the ethical tone of an organization and ensuring that ethical considerations are taken into account in AI projects.

This involves leading by example, promoting a culture of ethical awareness, and encouraging open and honest discussions about the ethical implications of AI. It also involves holding individuals and teams accountable for their actions and ensuring that ethical breaches are dealt with appropriately.

Conclusion: The Way Forward for Ethical AI

Navigating the ethical AI landscape is a complex and ongoing process. It requires a combination of tools and resources, ethics training and education, and ethical leadership.

As we move forward, it's crucial to continue the conversation about ethical AI and to keep questioning, learning, and adapting. Only by doing so can we ensure that AI is developed and used in a way that respects our ethical values and norms and contributes to a fair and just society.

In the next lesson, we'll delve deeper into the ethical dilemmas posed by AI and discuss strategies for ethical decision-making in AI.

"AI is not the end of the human story, but a new chapter full of unprecedented adventures." - Dennis Frank

9.9 Case Study: Ethical Dilemmas in AI

In this lesson, we will delve into a real-world case study that highlights the ethical dilemmas posed by AI. We will dissect the case, discuss the ethical issues it raises, analyze the decision-making process involved, and draw lessons from it.

Case Study: The Self-Driving Car Dilemma

Our case study revolves around self-driving cars, a prominent application of AI. Imagine a scenario where a self-driving car is about to crash, and it must decide between two options: swerve and hit a pedestrian or continue straight and hit a barrier, potentially harming the passenger. This is a classic example of an ethical dilemma in AI known as the "Trolley Problem."

Ethical Issues Raised

This case study raises several ethical issues:

1. **Value of Life**: Who should the car prioritize, the pedestrian or the passenger? This question brings up the issue of the value of life and how an AI system should be programmed to prioritize it.

2. **Accountability**: If an accident occurs, who is responsible? The AI, the car manufacturer, or the passenger who chose to use a self-driving car? This highlights the issue of accountability in AI.

3. **Transparency**: Should AI systems be transparent about how they make decisions in such scenarios? This brings up the issue of transparency in AI.

Decision-Making Process

In this case, the decision-making process is programmed by the AI developers. However, it's a complex task as it involves making ethical judgments. The developers must weigh the ethical implications of each decision and program the AI accordingly. This process also involves considering legal implications, societal norms, and public opinion.

Lessons Learned

From this case study, we can draw several lessons:

1. **Ethical Programming is Crucial**: AI developers must consider ethical implications when programming AI systems. They need to define clear ethical guidelines for AI decision-making.

2. **Transparency is Key**: AI systems should be transparent about their decision-making process to ensure accountability and foster trust.

3. **Public Involvement is Necessary**: The public should be involved in discussions about AI ethics, as these decisions impact society as a whole.

In conclusion, this case study underscores the importance of addressing ethical dilemmas in AI. As AI continues to evolve, we must navigate these moral mazes with care, ensuring that AI serves humanity while respecting ethical norms.

9.10 The Future of Ethical AI

Predictions for the Future of Ethical AI

As we move forward into an increasingly AI-driven world, the importance of ethical AI cannot be overstated. The future of ethical AI is likely to be shaped by several key trends. Firstly, we can expect a greater emphasis on transparency. As AI systems become more complex, understanding how they make decisions will become ever more crucial. We can anticipate advancements in explainable AI, which aims to make AI decision-making processes more transparent and understandable.

Secondly, we can expect increased regulation. As the implications of AI become more apparent, governments and organizations will likely implement more comprehensive regulations to ensure ethical practices in AI development and use.

Thirdly, we may see a shift towards more human-centric AI. This involves designing AI systems that prioritize human values and wellbeing, ensuring that AI benefits all of humanity and not just a select few.

The Role of Emerging Technologies in Ethical AI

Emerging technologies will play a crucial role in shaping the future of ethical AI. Technologies like blockchain could provide a secure and transparent framework for AI operations, ensuring accountability and trust in AI systems.

On the other hand, advancements in machine learning techniques could lead to more fair and unbiased AI systems. For instance, techniques like federated learning can help protect privacy while still allowing AI systems to learn from a vast amount of data.

The Potential Impact of Ethical AI on Society and Individuals

The potential impact of ethical AI on society and individuals is profound. Ethical AI has the potential to create a more equitable and just society. By ensuring that AI systems are fair, transparent, and accountable, we can prevent harmful biases and discrimination that can arise from AI decision-making.

On an individual level, ethical AI can protect our rights and freedoms. It can ensure that our data is used responsibly and that we are not unfairly targeted or discriminated against by AI systems.

Conclusion: The Importance of Ethical AI in the AI-Driven Future

In conclusion, ethical AI is not just a nice-to-have, but a must-have in our AI-driven future. As AI becomes more integrated into our lives, ensuring that it is used ethically will be crucial for protecting our rights, promoting fairness, and creating a more equitable society.

The future of ethical AI is bright, but it requires our active engagement. By staying informed, advocating for transparency and accountability, and pushing for regulations that protect our rights, we can help shape a future where AI serves all of humanity.

"In the hands of the wise, AI is a tool for building a future that respects and enhances human dignity."
- Dennis Frank

10.1 Embracing the AI-Driven Future

Understanding the AI-Driven Future

The future is AI-driven. It's not a matter of if, but when. Artificial Intelligence (AI) is already revolutionizing various sectors, from healthcare to finance, retail to education, and beyond. It's changing the way we live, work, and interact with the world.

AI is not just about robots and automation. It's about intelligent systems that can learn, adapt, and make decisions. It's about data-driven insights that can help us make better decisions and solve complex problems. It's about enhancing human capabilities, not replacing them.

But what does an AI-driven future look like? It's a future where AI is embedded in every aspect of our lives. It's a future where AI helps us make smarter decisions, improves our health, enhances our learning, and makes our lives more convenient and efficient. It's a future where AI helps us tackle some of the biggest challenges facing our world, from climate change to poverty.

The Importance of Adapting to AI

Adapting to the AI-driven future is not just important, it's essential. As AI continues to evolve and permeate every aspect of our lives, those who fail to adapt risk being left behind.

Adapting to AI means understanding its potential and its limitations. It means learning new skills and embracing new ways of thinking. It means being open to change and willing to take risks. It means recognizing the ethical implications of AI and navigating them with care.

Adapting to AI also means recognizing its potential to create new opportunities. AI is not just about job displacement, it's also about job creation. It's about new industries, new professions, and new ways of working. It's about leveraging AI to enhance our capabilities and expand our possibilities.

Strategies for Embracing AI in Everyday Life

So, how can we embrace the AI-driven future? Here are some strategies:

1. **Educate Yourself**: Learn about AI, its applications, and its implications. Understand how it works, what it can do, and what it can't do. Stay informed about the latest developments in AI.

2. **Develop New Skills**: As AI reshapes the job market, new skills will be in demand. Skills like data analysis, machine learning, and AI ethics will become increasingly important. Look for opportunities to develop these skills, whether through formal education, online courses, or self-study.

3. **Leverage AI Tools**: There are many AI tools and applications available today, from personal assistants to recommendation engines. Use these tools to make your life more convenient and efficient.

4. **Participate in the AI Conversation**: AI is not just a technical issue, it's a societal issue. Participate in the

conversation about AI. Share your thoughts and concerns. Advocate for ethical and responsible use of AI.

5. **Adopt a Growth Mindset**: Embracing the AI-driven future requires a growth mindset. It requires the willingness to learn, adapt, and grow. It requires the courage to embrace change, take risks, and explore new possibilities.

Embracing the AI-driven future is not just about surviving, it's about thriving. It's about leveraging AI to enhance our lives, expand our possibilities, and create a better future for all.

"The future is already here — it's just not very evenly distributed."
– William Gibson

10.2 Lifelong Learning in the AI Era

The Importance of Lifelong Learning in the AI Era

In the era of Artificial Intelligence (AI), the landscape of knowledge and skills is evolving at an unprecedented pace. The jobs and tasks that were once considered secure are being automated, and new roles are emerging that require a different set of skills. This rapid transformation necessitates a culture of lifelong learning.

Lifelong learning is the ongoing, voluntary, and self-motivated pursuit of knowledge for personal or professional reasons. In the context of the AI era, lifelong learning is not just a tool for personal development, but a necessity for survival in the job market. It is the key to staying relevant, competitive, and innovative in a world that is increasingly driven by AI.

Strategies for Continuous Learning and Development

To thrive in the AI era, it's essential to adopt strategies for continuous learning and development. Here are some strategies that can help:

1. **Embrace a Growth Mindset**: This mindset is about believing that your abilities can be developed through

dedication and hard work. It's about being open to new ideas, challenges, and feedback.

2. **Stay Curious**: Curiosity fuels learning. Stay informed about the latest trends and developments in AI and related fields. Attend seminars, webinars, and conferences. Read books, articles, and research papers.

3. **Learn by Doing**: Practical application of knowledge enhances understanding and retention. Participate in projects, internships, or part-time jobs that allow you to apply what you've learned.

4. **Leverage Online Learning Platforms**: Online learning platforms offer a vast array of courses on AI and related fields. These platforms allow you to learn at your own pace and according to your own schedule.

5. **Network with Like-Minded Individuals**: Engage with communities of learners and professionals in AI. Networking can provide you with valuable insights, feedback, and opportunities.

Case Study: Lifelong Learners Thriving in the AI Era

Let's look at a case study that illustrates the power of lifelong learning in the AI era.

John, a bank teller, noticed that his job was being automated. Instead of resisting the change, he embraced it. He started learning about AI and its applications in banking. He took online courses, participated in webinars, and networked with AI professionals.

His continuous learning paid off when his bank decided to implement an AI-based customer service system. Thanks to his newly acquired knowledge and skills, John was able to transition to a new role as an AI customer service specialist.

This case study shows that lifelong learning can help individuals adapt to the AI-driven changes in their careers and thrive in the AI era.

In conclusion, the AI era presents both challenges and opportunities. By embracing lifelong learning, we can navigate these challenges, seize the opportunities, and thrive in the AI era. Remember, in the world of AI, learning never stops.

"Artificial intelligence will be part of the home just like the light bulb." - Colin Angle

10.3 AI and the Changing Job Market

As we dig deeper into the AI era, it's crucial to understand how this technology is transforming the job market. AI is not just a tool that automates tasks; it's a disruptive force that's reshaping industries and redefining roles. This lesson will help you understand these changes and equip you with strategies to stay relevant in an AI-driven job market.

Understanding How AI is Transforming the Job Market

AI's impact on the job market is multifaceted and profound. It's not just about job displacement due to automation; it's also about job transformation and creation. AI automates repetitive and mundane tasks, freeing up humans to focus on more complex and creative tasks. It's also creating new roles that didn't exist before, such as AI ethicists and data scientists.

However, the transition isn't always smooth. Some jobs are at risk of becoming obsolete, and there's a growing skills gap as the demand for AI-related skills outpaces supply. It's also worth noting that the impact of AI varies across industries and regions. Some sectors, such as manufacturing and transportation, are more susceptible to automation than others.

Adapting to AI-Driven Changes in the Job Market

Adapting to the AI-driven changes in the job market requires a proactive and flexible approach. Here are some strategies to consider:

1. **Continuous Learning**: AI is a rapidly evolving field. Staying updated with the latest developments and trends is essential. This could involve taking online courses, attending webinars, or reading AI-related publications.

2. **Skills Development**: Acquiring AI-related skills, such as data analysis, machine learning, and programming, can increase your employability. However, don't neglect soft skills like critical thinking, creativity, and emotional intelligence. These skills are less susceptible to automation and are increasingly valued in the AI era.

3. **Career Planning**: As AI reshapes the job market, some roles may become less relevant, while others gain importance. Regularly reassess your career path and be open to pivoting if necessary.

4. **Networking**: Connect with professionals in the AI field. They can provide valuable insights, advice, and opportunities.

Strategies for Staying Relevant in an AI-Driven Job Market

Staying relevant in an AI-driven job market is about more than just surviving; it's about thriving. Here are some strategies to help you do just that:

1. **Embrace AI**: Rather than fearing AI, see it as a tool that can enhance your work. Learn how to use AI applications relevant to your field and explore ways to integrate them into your work processes.

2. **Leverage Your Unique Strengths**: AI is excellent at crunching numbers and following algorithms, but it lacks human qualities like empathy, intuition, and creativity. Leverage these unique human strengths.

3. **Adopt a Growth Mindset**: In the AI era, change is the only constant. Adopt a growth mindset that embraces change and views challenges as opportunities for learning and growth.

By understanding the changes AI brings to the job market and adopting the right strategies, you can not only adapt but thrive in the AI era. The future of work is here, and it's AI-driven. Embrace the change and seize the opportunities it brings.

"Technology, like art, is a soaring exercise of the human imagination."
- Daniel Bell

10.4 AI and the Evolution of Skills

The Evolving Skill Set Required in the AI Era

In the AI era, the skill sets required are evolving rapidly. Traditional skills are being replaced by new ones, and this shift is happening across all industries. With AI systems taking over repetitive and mundane tasks, the demand for cognitive and emotional skills is on the rise.

AI is not just about coding and data analysis, it's also about understanding how to leverage AI tools effectively, problem-solving, creativity, and adaptability. The ability to learn and adapt quickly is becoming more valuable than ever.

Strategies for Acquiring and Developing New Skills

Adapting to the AI era requires a proactive approach to learning. Here are some strategies to help you acquire and develop new skills:

1. **Continuous Learning**: The AI era is marked by rapid changes, making lifelong learning crucial. Embrace online learning platforms, webinars, workshops, and other resources to keep up with the latest trends and developments.

2. **Hands-On Experience**: Practical experience is invaluable. Try to get hands-on experience with AI tools and platforms. Many AI tools offer free trials, which you can use to gain practical experience.

3. **Networking**: Connect with professionals in the field. Attend AI-related events and join online communities. This can provide insights into the latest trends and opportunities.

4. **Mentorship**: Seek mentorship from professionals in the field. They can provide guidance and insights that can help you navigate your learning journey.

Case Study: Skill Evolution in the Tech Industry

The tech industry is at the forefront of the AI revolution and provides a clear example of how skills are evolving. In the past, knowledge of specific programming languages was highly sought after. Today, while technical skills remain important, there's an increasing demand for skills like data analysis, machine learning, and AI ethics.

Moreover, soft skills such as problem-solving, creativity, and communication are becoming increasingly important. Tech companies are looking for individuals who can not only develop AI systems but also understand their implications and communicate their benefits and risks effectively.

In conclusion, the AI era is transforming the skill sets required in the job market. By embracing continuous learning and seeking practical experience, we can adapt to these changes and thrive in the AI era.

10.5 AI and the Transformation of Industries

Artificial Intelligence (AI) is not just a futuristic concept; it's a present reality that is reshaping various industries. From healthcare and finance to retail and education, AI is transforming traditional operations and creating new paradigms. In this lesson, we will explore how AI is revolutionizing industries and discuss strategies for adapting to these AI-driven changes.

Understanding How AI is Transforming Various Industries

AI's transformative impact is being felt across various sectors. Here's a brief overview:

- **Healthcare**: AI is being used to improve diagnosis, treatment planning, patient care, and administrative tasks. Machine learning algorithms can analyze complex medical data to identify patterns that humans might miss, leading to more accurate diagnoses and personalized treatment plans.

- **Finance**: AI is reshaping the finance industry by automating tasks like fraud detection, risk assessment, and customer service. AI-powered robo-advisors are providing personalized investment advice, making wealth management accessible to more people.

- **Retail**: AI is revolutionizing the retail industry by enhancing customer experiences through personalized recommendations and predictive analytics for inventory management.

- **Education**: AI is transforming education by enabling personalized learning, automating grading, and providing insights to improve teaching methods.

Strategies for Adapting to AI-Driven Changes in Your Industry

As AI continues to transform industries, it's crucial to adapt to stay relevant. Here are some strategies:

1. **Stay Informed**: Keep up to date with the latest AI trends and developments in your industry.

2. **Upskill and Reskill**: Acquire new skills relevant to AI applications in your field. This could involve learning about machine learning, data analysis, or AI ethics.

3. **Embrace Change**: Be open to new ways of working and be ready to adapt your processes and strategies as AI continues to evolve.

4. **Collaborate with AI**: View AI as a tool that can enhance your work rather than replace it. Learn how to work effectively with AI systems.

Case Study: Industry Transformation in Healthcare

AI's impact on healthcare is profound and far-reaching. Let's look at a case study:

PathAI is a company that uses AI to assist pathologists in diagnosing diseases from medical images. Their AI-powered system can analyze slides more quickly and accurately than humans, leading to faster diagnoses and treatment plans. This not only improves patient outcomes but also reduces the workload for overburdened pathologists.

AI is transforming healthcare by automating routine tasks, improving diagnoses, personalizing treatment plans, and enhancing patient care. As AI continues to advance, we can expect even more significant transformations in the healthcare industry.

In conclusion, AI is transforming industries at an unprecedented pace. By staying informed, upskilling, embracing change, and learning to collaborate with AI, you can adapt and thrive in this AI-driven future.

"AI is not just a technological revolution; it's a cultural and philosophical renaissance." - Dennis Frank

10.6 AI and the Future of Work

Welcome to Lesson 10.6, where we will delve into the future of work in the AI era, discuss how to adapt to AI-driven changes in the workplace, and explore strategies for thriving in the future of work.

The Future of Work in the AI Era

The advent of AI is set to revolutionize the workplace, ushering in a new era of work. AI, with its ability to automate routine tasks, analyze vast amounts of data, and learn from experience, is poised to transform many professions.

AI will not only change the nature of work but also the structure of the workplace. We can expect more remote and flexible work arrangements as AI-powered tools make collaboration and communication more efficient. We might also see a shift towards project-based work as AI enables more efficient project management.

However, the AI revolution will not be without its challenges. Jobs that involve routine tasks are at risk of being automated. There might also be a skills gap as the demand for AI-related skills outstrips supply.

Adapting to AI-Driven Changes in the Workplace

Adapting to the AI-driven changes in the workplace will require both individuals and organizations to be proactive.

For individuals, lifelong learning will be crucial. As AI transforms the job market, the demand for AI-related skills will increase. Individuals will need to continually update their skills to stay relevant. This could involve learning new technical skills, such as programming and data analysis, as well as soft skills, like creativity and emotional intelligence, which are less likely to be automated.

For organizations, adapting to AI will involve rethinking their business models and processes. They will need to invest in AI technologies and training for their employees. They might also need to rethink their hiring strategies to attract talent with the necessary AI skills.

Strategies for Thriving in the Future of Work

Thriving in the future of work will require a growth mindset and a willingness to adapt. Here are a few strategies:

1. **Embrace Lifelong Learning**: As mentioned earlier, the demand for AI-related skills will increase. Embrace lifelong learning to keep your skills up-to-date.

2. **Cultivate Soft Skills**: While AI can automate many tasks, there are skills it can't replicate, such as creativity, leadership, and emotional intelligence. Cultivating these skills can give you an edge in the AI-driven job market.

3. **Stay Informed**: Keep up with the latest trends and developments in AI. This can help you anticipate changes in the job market and adapt accordingly.

4. **Network**: Build relationships with people in your industry. They can provide valuable insights and opportunities.

5. **Be Flexible**: Be open to new ways of working. This could involve working remotely, collaborating with AI, or taking on project-based work.

In conclusion, the AI revolution is set to transform the workplace. By understanding these changes and adopting the right strategies, you can not only adapt but thrive in the future of work. In the next lesson, we will explore how AI is driving the evolution of society.

"In the realm of AI, every step forward is a step towards understanding ourselves better." - Dennis Frank

10.7 AI and the Evolution of Society

Understanding how AI is Transforming Society

Artificial Intelligence (AI) is not just a technological revolution, but it's also a societal one. It's transforming the way we live, work, and interact with the world around us. From autonomous vehicles and smart homes to personalized recommendations and virtual assistants, AI is becoming an integral part of our daily lives.

The impact of AI on society is profound and multifaceted. It's changing the way we communicate, learn, and make decisions. It's influencing our social norms, economic structures, and political systems. It's reshaping our industries, creating new jobs while making others obsolete. It's even challenging our ethical and moral frameworks, raising questions about privacy, fairness, and accountability.

The Role of Individuals in an AI-driven Society

In an AI-driven society, every individual has a role to play. As consumers, we are the end-users of AI technologies, benefiting from their convenience, efficiency, and personalization. As workers, we need to adapt to the changing job market, acquiring new skills and embracing lifelong learning. As citizens, we have a voice in shaping the policies and regulations that govern the use of AI.

Moreover, we have a responsibility to use AI ethically and responsibly. This includes respecting others' privacy, combating AI bias and discrimination, and promoting transparency and accountability in AI systems. We also need to stay informed about the latest AI developments and their societal implications, making informed decisions about the use of AI in our lives.

Strategies for Contributing to an AI-driven Society

There are several strategies that individuals can adopt to contribute positively to an AI-driven society.

Education and Lifelong Learning: As AI continues to evolve, it's crucial to keep up with the latest developments and trends. This involves continuous learning and upskilling, not just in technical areas like data science and machine learning, but also in areas like ethics, law, and social sciences that are crucial for understanding the societal implications of AI.

Ethical Use of AI: Individuals can contribute to an AI-driven society by using AI technologies ethically and responsibly. This includes respecting privacy, combating AI bias, and promoting transparency and accountability.

Advocacy and Policy Engagement: Individuals can also engage in advocacy and policy discussions related to AI. This could involve participating in public consultations, joining advocacy groups, or even running for public office.

Innovation and Entrepreneurship: Finally, individuals can contribute to an AI-driven society by innovating and creating new AI solutions. This could involve starting a tech startup, developing an AI app, or conducting AI research.

In conclusion, adapting to an AI-driven society is not just about understanding AI technologies, but also about understanding their societal implications and our role in shaping them. By adopting the right strategies, we can all contribute to a future where AI is used for the benefit of all.

"The future of AI is a canvas of possibilities, where our most imaginative dreams can become realities."
- Dennis Frank

10.8 AI and the Future of Education

As we navigate through the AI era, it's crucial to understand how this technology is shaping the future of education and how we can adapt to these changes. This lesson will also provide strategies for lifelong learning in the AI era.

The Future of Education in the AI Era

Artificial Intelligence is transforming the education sector in unprecedented ways. From personalized learning experiences to efficient administrative tasks, AI is revolutionizing how education is delivered and received.

AI-powered systems can adapt to individual learning styles, providing personalized content and resources to enhance the learning process. For instance, AI can identify areas where a student is struggling and provide additional resources to help them improve.

Furthermore, AI is also being used to automate administrative tasks such as grading and scheduling, freeing up time for educators to focus on teaching and mentoring.

In the future, we can expect AI to play an even larger role in education. We might see more sophisticated AI tutors capable of providing comprehensive and personalized education to students, regardless of their location. AI could also be used to predict future learning outcomes and career paths, helping students make informed decisions about their education and career.

Adapting to AI-Driven Changes in Education

As AI continues to reshape the educational landscape, it's important for educators, students, and parents to adapt to these changes.

For educators, this might mean learning how to use AI tools and integrating them into their teaching methods. They might also need to update their skills and knowledge to stay relevant in the AI-driven education sector.

For students, adapting to AI-driven changes in education might involve embracing new ways of learning. This could include using AI-powered learning platforms, participating in online classes, or learning from AI tutors.

Parents can also play a role in helping their children adapt to these changes. They can encourage their children to use AI tools for learning and provide support as they navigate the new educational landscape.

Strategies for Lifelong Learning in the AI Era

In the AI era, lifelong learning is more important than ever. As AI continues to evolve and influence various sectors, including education, the skills and knowledge required to succeed are also changing.

Here are some strategies for lifelong learning in the AI era:

1. **Stay Curious**: Embrace a mindset of continuous learning. Be curious about new technologies and how they can enhance your learning and career.

2. **Leverage AI Tools**: Use AI-powered tools and platforms to enhance your learning. These tools can provide personalized learning experiences and help you learn at your own pace.

3. **Update Your Skills**: As AI reshapes various sectors, the skills required to succeed are also changing. Stay relevant by updating your skills and learning about new technologies.

4. **Network**: Connect with others in your field. Share knowledge, learn from others, and stay updated on the latest trends and developments in AI.

5. **Embrace Change**: The AI era is characterized by rapid changes. Embrace these changes and see them as opportunities for growth and learning.

In conclusion, AI is transforming the future of education, and it's crucial for us to adapt to these changes. By embracing lifelong learning and leveraging AI tools, we can thrive in the AI era. In the next lesson, we'll explore how AI is reshaping the entertainment industry.

10.9 AI and the Future of Entertainment

The Future of Entertainment in the AI Era

Artificial Intelligence (AI) is poised to revolutionize the entertainment industry in unprecedented ways, and we are only just beginning to see the potential of this technology. AI is not only transforming how content is created, but also how it's consumed and distributed.

AI algorithms are now capable of creating music, writing scripts, and even producing short films. These advancements are pushing the boundaries of creativity and opening new possibilities for artists and creators.

On the consumption side, AI is enhancing personalization like never before. Recommendation systems powered by AI are becoming increasingly sophisticated, delivering content that aligns with individual tastes and preferences. This level of personalization is changing the way audiences engage with entertainment, creating a more immersive and tailored experience.

AI is also playing a significant role in content distribution. With the rise of streaming platforms, AI is being used to optimize content delivery, ensuring a seamless and high-quality viewing experience.

Adapting to AI-Driven Changes in Entertainment

As AI continues to reshape the entertainment landscape, it's essential to adapt and stay ahead of these changes. Whether you're a content creator, a consumer, or a professional in the entertainment industry, understanding the implications of AI is crucial.

For creators, embracing AI can open new avenues for creativity and innovation. While AI can automate certain aspects of content creation, it doesn't replace the need for human creativity. Instead, it serves as a tool that can enhance and augment creative processes.

For consumers, adapting to AI-driven entertainment means embracing personalization and interactivity. Engaging with AI-powered platforms can enhance your entertainment experience, providing you with content that aligns with your preferences and viewing habits.

Professionals in the entertainment industry need to understand how AI is transforming their field. This includes staying updated on the latest AI trends and technologies, and understanding how these changes can impact business models, revenue streams, and audience engagement.

Strategies for Engaging with AI-Driven Entertainment

Engaging with AI-driven entertainment can be a rewarding experience, provided you approach it with the right strategies. Here are a few tips:

- **Embrace Personalization**: AI-powered recommendation systems can enhance your entertainment experience by delivering content tailored to your preferences. Don't shy away from these personalized experiences but embrace them.

- **Stay Informed**: Keep yourself updated about the latest developments in AI and entertainment. This will help you understand how AI is shaping the entertainment landscape and how you can make the most of these changes.

- **Be Open to New Experiences**: AI is pushing the boundaries of what's possible in entertainment. Be open to these new experiences, whether it's an AI-generated song or a film scripted by an AI.

- **Understand the Implications**: While AI is transforming entertainment, it's also raising important ethical and privacy concerns. It's important to understand these implications and make informed decisions about the AI-driven entertainment you engage with.

In conclusion, the future of entertainment in the AI era is exciting and full of potential. By understanding these changes and adapting accordingly, you can thrive in this new landscape and make the most of the AI-driven entertainment revolution.

10.10 Thriving in the AI Era

Welcome to the final lesson of our comprehensive course on Artificial Intelligence. We've come a long way, exploring the intricate world of AI and its implications across various sectors. Now, let's focus on how we can thrive in this AI-driven era.

Strategies for Thriving in the AI Era

Living in the age of AI requires a fresh mindset and a new set of skills. Here are some strategies to help you thrive:

1. Embrace Lifelong Learning: AI is a rapidly evolving field. To stay relevant, we must commit to continuous learning. This doesn't necessarily mean going back to school, but rather taking advantage of online courses, webinars, and workshops to keep up with the latest developments in AI.

2. Cultivate a Growth Mindset: A growth mindset, as opposed to a fixed mindset, is crucial in the AI era. This means seeing challenges as opportunities for growth and understanding that effort is a necessary path to mastery.

3. Develop AI Fluency: Even if you're not a tech professional, it's important to have a basic understanding of AI. This includes knowing the terminology, understanding how AI can be applied in your field, and staying informed about ethical and societal implications of AI.

4. Foster Creativity and Emotional Intelligence: While AI can automate many tasks, it can't replicate human creativity and emotional intelligence. These skills will become increasingly valuable in the AI era.

The Importance of Resilience and Adaptability in the AI Era

In the AI era, change is the only constant. As AI continues to evolve and disrupt industries, jobs that exist today may be automated tomorrow. This can be unsettling, but it also presents opportunities for those who are adaptable and resilient.

Resilience is about bouncing back from challenges and setbacks. In the context of AI, this could mean learning new skills when your job is automated or finding new ways to add value in your role as AI takes over certain tasks.

Adaptability, on the other hand, is about being flexible and willing to change. This could mean shifting your career path, embracing new technologies, or learning to work alongside AI.

Conclusion: Embracing the AI-Driven Future

The AI era is here, and it's transforming the way we live and work. While this can be intimidating, it's also an exciting time of innovation and opportunity. By embracing lifelong learning, cultivating a growth mindset, developing AI fluency, and fostering creativity and emotional intelligence, we can not only adapt but thrive in this AI-driven future.

Remember, the future is not something that happens to us. It's something we create. So, let's embrace the AI revolution and shape a future where technology enhances our lives, rather than dictates them.

Thank you for joining us on this journey through the world of AI. We hope this course has given you valuable insights and tools to navigate and thrive in the AI era. Keep learning, stay curious, and remember: the future is in your hands.

"AI's potential is like a seed; our guidance and ethics are the soil in which it will flourish." - Dennis Frank

GLOSSARY of AI TERMS

Adaptive Learning Systems: Software that adjusts content and teaching methods based on individual learner's needs and performance.

Administrative Tasks Automation: Use of software or AI to automate routine office tasks like scheduling, data entry, or email management.

AI and Copyright: Concerns about intellectual property rights in works created by or with the assistance of artificial intelligence.

AI and Data Privacy Laws: Legal considerations and regulations concerning the handling of personal data by AI systems.

AI and Human Rights: The impact of AI technologies on human rights, such as privacy, freedom of expression, and non-discrimination.

AI and Project-Based Work: The integration of AI tools in managing and executing project tasks, enhancing efficiency and decision-making.

AI Bias Mitigation Strategies: Methods to reduce or eliminate bias in AI systems, ensuring fairness and impartiality in decision-making.

AI Driven Content Creation: Use of AI to generate digital content such as text, images, or music.

AI Driven Feedback: Automated feedback systems powered by AI, providing personalized insights and assessments.

AI Driven Monetization Strategies: Business models and strategies leveraging AI for revenue generation and profit maximization.

AI Ethics Committees: Groups responsible for overseeing the ethical implications and practices of AI within an organization.

AI Ethics Officers: Professionals specializing in guiding and enforcing ethical AI practices and policies.

AI Ethics Policy Development: The process of creating guidelines and standards to govern ethical AI development and use.

AI Ethics Training: Education programs focusing on the ethical aspects and implications of AI technology.

AI Impact on Privacy and Security: The effects of AI on individual privacy and data security, including risks and protections.

AI in Creativity: The role of AI in enhancing or facilitating creative processes in arts, design, and other creative fields.

AI in Curriculum Development: The integration of AI tools in designing educational curricula, tailored to individual learning needs.

AI in Gaming: The application of AI in video games for tasks like game design, NPC behavior, or dynamic content generation.

AI in Social Justice: The use of AI in promoting fairness, equality, and justice in social contexts.

AI in Student Assessment: Utilizing AI for evaluating student performance and learning progress.

AI Tools in Education: Various AI technologies applied in educational settings for teaching, learning, and administration.

Algorithmic Composition: The process of creating music or art using algorithms, often with the aid of AI.

Anomaly Detection in Medical Scans: The use of AI to identify abnormalities in medical imaging that may indicate disease or injury.

Artificial Intelligence (AI): The simulation of human intelligence processes by machines, especially computer systems.

Augmented Reality (AR): An interactive experience where real-world environments are enhanced by computer-generated perceptual information.

Behavioral Algorithms: Computer algorithms designed to predict, analyze, or respond to human behavior.

Bias in AI Systems: The presence of prejudice or unfairness in AI algorithms, often reflecting biases in training data.

Chatbots: AI-powered software that can simulate conversation with human users, especially over the internet.

ChatGPT: An AI language model developed by OpenAI, capable of understanding and generating human-like text.

Consequentialism in AI: An ethical framework in AI focusing on the consequences or outcomes of AI actions or decisions.

Course Design with AI: The use of AI tools to create and structure educational courses.

Creative Paradigm: A framework or model that guides creative processes, potentially influenced by AI technologies.

Credit Score Analysis: AI systems analyzing credit data to determine creditworthiness and risk.

Customer Service Automation: Using AI and other technologies to automate customer service tasks like answering queries or resolving issues.

Data (in AI context): Information used by AI systems for training, learning, and making decisions.

Data-Driven Decision Making: Making decisions based on data analysis and interpretation, often using AI and machine learning.

Data-Driven Insights: Understandings or findings derived from the analysis of data, particularly through AI algorithms.

Deontological Ethics in AI: An ethical approach in AI focused on adherence to rules, duties, or obligations.

Digital Literacy in AI: The ability to understand, use, and interact with AI and digital technologies effectively.

Dynamic Learning Environments: Educational settings that adapt and change in response to learners' needs, often using AI.

Dynamic Game Environments: Video game settings that change or adapt in response to player actions, often through AI.

Educational Evolution: The ongoing changes and advancements in education, including the integration of AI technologies.

Ethical AI: AI developed and used in a manner that adheres to moral and ethical standards.

Ethical Considerations in AI Education: The study of moral and ethical implications related to teaching and learning about AI.

Ethical Decision-Making Frameworks: Structures or models guiding ethical choices and actions, particularly in AI contexts.

Ethical Implications of AI: The moral consequences and considerations associated with the development and use of AI.

Ethical Leadership in AI: Leading AI initiatives or organizations with a focus on maintaining ethical standards.

Ethical AI Design: The process of creating AI systems with consideration for ethical principles and impacts.

Facial Recognition: A technology capable of identifying or verifying a person from a digital image or video frame using AI.

Financial Planning: The process of managing finances, often assisted by AI, to meet personal or business objectives.

Game Design: The art and science of creating the rules and content of games, increasingly utilizing AI.

Healthcare AI: AI applications in healthcare, such as diagnostics, treatment planning, and patient care.

Home Automation Systems: Systems that control lighting, climate, entertainment systems, and appliances in a home, often using AI.

Inclusion in AI Development: Ensuring diverse perspectives and representation in the creation of AI systems.

Inclusive Learning Environments: Educational settings designed to be accessible and accommodating to all learners.

Intelligent Systems: Systems that can perceive, reason, learn, and act intelligently, often through AI technologies.

Intelligent Tutoring Systems: Computer systems that provide personalized instruction or feedback to learners, typically using AI.

Interactive Entertainment: Entertainment experiences that are interactive, often using AI, such as video games or virtual reality.

Inventory Management: The supervision and control of the ordering, storage, and use of components that a company will use in the production of items it will sell or the amount of stock items it will sell.

Investing Strategies: Approaches to investing in financial assets, increasingly informed by AI and data analysis.

Liability in Healthcare AI: Legal responsibility and accountability issues associated with the use of AI in healthcare.

Machine Learning (ML): A subset of AI focused on algorithms and statistical models that enable computers to learn from and make decisions based on data.

Market Analysis: The study of market conditions to identify opportunities and risks, often using AI tools for enhanced insights.

Music Production: The process of creating, composing, recording, and producing music, with increasing use of AI technologies.

Neural Networks: Computational models inspired by the human brain, used in AI for pattern recognition and decision-making.

Non-Player Characters (NPCs): Characters in a video game that are not controlled by a player but by AI.

Personalized Playlists: Music or media playlists tailored to individual preferences, often created using AI algorithms.

Predictive Analytics: The use of data, statistical algorithms, and AI techniques to identify the likelihood of future outcomes.

Predictive Health Risks: AI-driven analysis of medical data to predict future health risks for individuals.

Predictive Search: Search systems that anticipate the user's needs and provide suggestions, using AI algorithms.

Predictive Trends: Forecasting future trends or patterns based on current data, often using AI.

Privacy and Data Security: The protection of personal data and privacy in the context of AI and digital technologies.

Real-Time Data Analysis: The immediate processing and analysis of data as it's collected, often using AI for timely insights.

Recommendation Systems: AI-based systems that suggest products, services, or content to users based on their preferences and behavior.

Reinforcement Learning: An area of machine learning where an AI learns to make decisions by trial and error, receiving feedback from its environment.

Retirement Planning: The process of determining retirement income goals and the actions necessary to achieve them, often using AI for analysis and advice.

Robo-advisors: Automated platforms that provide financial advice and investment management online with minimal human intervention, using AI algorithms.

Smart Cities: Urban areas that use various forms of electronic data collection sensors to supply information used to manage assets and resources efficiently.

Telemedicine: The use of telecommunication and information technology to provide clinical health care from a distance, often incorporating AI for diagnostics and patient management.

Testing Data: Data used to evaluate the performance of AI models, separate from training data.

Training Data: Data used to train AI models, teaching them to make predictions or perform tasks.

Validation Data: Data used to fine-tune and validate AI models, ensuring their accuracy and effectiveness.

Virtual Assistants (e.g., Siri, Alexa, Google Assistant): AI-powered software programs that assist users with tasks like setting reminders, answering questions, and controlling smart devices, typically through voice commands.

Virtual Health Assistants: Digital tools, often powered by AI, designed to provide health-related assistance, such as monitoring health metrics, offering medical advice, or reminding users to take their medication.

Virtual Influencers: Digitally-created characters or entities, often with AI-driven personalities, used in social media and marketing to influence audiences. They can interact with followers, promote products, and create content similar to human influencers.

Virtual Reality (VR): A simulated experience that can be similar to or completely different from the real world, typically achieved through VR headsets. It immerses users in a fully digital environment, often used for gaming, training, education, or entertainment.

Meet the Course Creator

Dennis Frank, a seasoned veteran of the mining industry, transitioned from a 43-year career to pursue his passion for the digital world, focusing on website development and content creation in the realms of AI, cryptocurrency and blockchain. Dennis's journey is a testament to his belief in continuous learning and adaptation.

Originally a music major at the University of Northern Colorado (UNC), Dennis's love for the arts seamlessly blends with his technical acumen. His curiosity and dedication to understanding the intricacies of AI, blockchain and cryptocurrency have given him a voice in the digital community.

From the Mines to the Digital World

Dennis's transition from mining to digital content creation symbolizes a bridge between traditional industries and the burgeoning world of AI technology. His approach to explaining complex concepts in AI is deeply rooted in his own journey of discovery and education, making his content relatable and easy to understand.

Published Works

- **Mastering Tokenomics: The Ultimate Guide** – A comprehensive exploration of digital tokens and their impact on the economy, ideated and compiled by Dennis to simplify the world of blockchain for enthusiasts and professionals alike.

- **AI Unveiled: Navigating the Intersection of Technology, Ethics, and Society** – This book demystifies AI, breaking it down into understandable components, emphasizing that AI is not just about replicating human intelligence but about creating tools to assist in daily tasks, problem-solving, and fostering discoveries beyond our current capabilities.

- **Crypto Currency Investment Strategies: A Comprehensive Guide** - This book is an essential resource for beginners, offering a deep dive into the intricacies of cryptocurrency investment.

- **Blockchain Unlocked: Navigating the Digital Ledger Revolution** - This book demystifies the complex world of blockchain, offering readers a clear understanding of what it is, how it works, and why it's rapidly becoming one of the most significant technological advancements of our time.

Life Beyond Writing

When not immersed in the digital world, Dennis is an avid fisherman and camper, finding solace in the serene landscapes of northeast Wyoming. A guitar enthusiast, he enjoys playing and teaching music, sharing the joy of melodies just as he shares knowledge in technology.

Married to Eva for 47 years, and a proud father to David and Christina, Dennis values family above all. His involvement in praise and worship at his local church showcases his commitment to community and faith.

Connect with Dennis Frank

Stay in tune with Dennis's latest explorations in blockchain, cryptocurrency, AI, and more. Discover engaging articles, informative videos, and insightful podcasts, all designed to enlighten and educate.

- Website: KryptoKraken™.com

A Note from Dennis

"I've always believed that the best way to understand a subject is to teach it. Sharing my journey into the world of AI technology has been an enriching experience, and I hope my work helps demystify this fascinating field for others. Thank you for joining me on this journey of continuous learning and discovery. Here's to exploring new horizons and living life to its fullest!"

Support my work: paypal.me/kryptokraken

"In this moment of revelation, as the ethereal veil lifts, we witness the true essence of AI - not as an overbearing force, but as a guardian, holding our world in a balance of knowledge and empathy. This grand unveiling is not just of technology, but of a future where AI, in its majestic complexity, intertwines with the very fabric of our lives. Here we see AI as a mirror, reflecting our diversity and shaping our destiny. Let us step into this new epoch with respect and anticipation, embracing AI as a partner in our collective journey towards a harmonious and enlightened existence." - Dennis Frank, "AI Unveiled: Navigating the Intersection of Technology, Ethics, and Society."

www.ingramcontent.com/pod-product-compliance
Lightning Source LLC
LaVergne TN
LVHW051222050326
832903LV00028B/2215